Excel 365 for Beginners

EXCEL 365 ESSENTIALS - BOOK 1

M.L. HUMPHREY

CONTENTS

WHY LEARN EXCEL   1

DISCUSSION OF DIFFERENT OFFICE VERSIONS   3

WHAT THIS BOOK COVERS   7

APPEARANCE SETTINGS   9

BASIC TERMINOLOGY   15

ABSOLUTE BASICS   29

NAVIGATING EXCEL   41

INPUT DATA   49

COPY, PASTE, AND MOVE DATA   65

FORMULAS AND FUNCTIONS   81

FORMATTING   95

SORTING AND FILTERING   125

PRINTING   135

CONCLUSION   145

SHORTCUTS   149

CONTENTS (CONT.)

INDEX 153

ABOUT THE AUTHOR 159

Why Learn Excel

Excel is great. I use it both in my professional life and my personal life. It allows me to organize and track key information in a quick and easy manner and to automate a lot of the calculations I need.

I have a budget worksheet that I look at at least every few days to track whether my bills have been paid and how much I need to keep in my bank account and just where I am overall financially.

(Which I shared in *Excel for Budgeting* and which you can also purchase a blank version of via my Payhip store if you're interested. Links available at https://mlhumphrey.com/business-and-personal-finance/)

In my professional career I've used Excel in a number of ways, from analyzing a series of financial transactions to see if a customer was overcharged to performing a comparison of regulatory requirements across multiple jurisdictions.

It's also the quickest and easiest way I've ever found to take rows of raw data and create summaries of that data.

While Excel works best for storing numbers and performing calculations, it is also often a good choice for text-based analysis, especially if you want to be able to sort your text results or filter out and isolate certain entries.

Excel also has very widespread usage. Every single corporate environment I ever worked in used Microsoft Office. I was in banking, finance, and consulting and all of those fields tend to default to Microsoft Office products.

More creative fields tend more towards Apple products, but your bread and butter corporations are very much still users of Office. So learning Excel (and Word and PowerPoint) is an essential skill if you want to be employed in those types of companies.

At least for the foreseeable future. Big companies do not like change.

And honestly, the skills you learn using Microsoft Excel can be applied to similar programs. I use Numbers on my Mac when I need to open a spreadsheet and other than remembering to do Command instead of Control for my shortcuts they work much the same way.

So Excel is definitely worth learning. It will help you with your own life and your career.

Now, real quick, I want to discuss the three main versions of Microsoft Office so you understand where this book fits.

Discussion of Different Office Versions

At this present moment (December 2022), Microsoft Office offers essentially three products that all share the same core functionality.

There is a free version of Microsoft Office that is available online. You can get access to Word, Excel, PowerPoint, and a number of other Microsoft tools by signing up for a free Microsoft account.

We'll call this one Office on the Web.

It has basic functionality that will work for most users, I suspect. But it's also all online. If you have a file on your computer and want to work with it in the free version you have to upload it and store it in a OneDrive account. It also has limited functionality, so it's not going to give you the full range of options as the paid products that Microsoft offers.

Second, are the old-school versions. That's what I have spent the last thirty years or so using. These are static versions of Office that are locked into place at a point in time.

As I write this, the latest static, or as Microsoft likes to call them, "on premise", version of Microsoft Office is Office 2021. The original Office Essentials books I wrote used Office 2013 and I also published a series of titles on Office 2019, but there have been many other versions of Office over the years.

Each of the static versions of Office are released with Office functionality as it exists at that time. They're not supposed to update if there are improvements made later.

(Although I've noticed that they have language about making updates and that sometimes they do seem to make updates, perhaps for security reasons, because I will sometimes notice that my old familiar program isn't working the way it used to.)

But the appearance and tasks do seem to stay fixed.

For example, they changed the appearance of Office with the release of Office 2021, but neither of my laptops, one running Office 2013 and one running Office 2019, were impacted. Also, with Office 2021 it looks like they released the function XLOOKUP to replace VLOOKUP and HLOOKUP, but I didn't get access to it.

One of the disadvantages of working with one of the static or "on premise" versions of Office is that you don't get future improvements like that.

You also, because Microsoft really wants to push people towards their subscription model, are generally limited to having that static version on only one computer. If that computer dies, oh well, you have to buy it again for the next computer. You can't transfer it.

(Again, that's what they say, but when I logged onto my new laptop with my Microsoft account they were ready to let me use Office 2019 on it even though I'd bought it for my old computer. So maybe it's more one computer at a time even though that is not what the license says.)

The advantage to the static versions, though, and the reason I like them, is that they are stable. I buy Office 2019, I figure out how it works, and I'm done until my computer dies.

I don't have to worry that I log in and they've changed things on me overnight. I am not a user who is on the cutting edge who needs the latest and greatest. And I don't collaborate which is where a lot of their more recent improvements seem to be focused so the changes they are making are generally ones that I don't need.

I just want things to stay the same so I don't have to think about anything when I'm ready to work.

Also, I like the static versions because I pay my $300 (or whatever the cost is at the time) once and never have to pay again or worry about losing the ability to edit my files.

But there are good reasons to use the third product option, Office 365, which is the subscription version of Office and the subject of this book.

One is that you can have access to Office across multiple devices. I have a few laptops and having Office 365, if I buy the right option, lets me have Office on my Mac as well as all of my laptops for one monthly fee.

If you're part of a family who all need access that can be a much cheaper option than paying to put Office on each computer.

Also, if everyone is using Office 365 then you know that everyone will be on the same page in terms of compatibility. One of the issues that I ran into professionally a number of years ago was that I was using a newer version of Office than one of my clients. I designed an entire workbook for them that did very complex calculations only to find out that they couldn't use the workbook because the Excel functions I relied on weren't available in the version of Office they were using. I had to redo the whole thing because they couldn't upgrade.

(Of course, that means that if you are going to use Office 365 or even Office 2021, and you're working with someone outside of your organization, you need to be very careful that you don't use something available to you (like XLOOKUP or TEXTJOIN) that that person can't use because they're using an older version of Office.)

Office 365 can also be far more portable if you're willing to put files on OneDrive. (I am not, because I'm a Luddite at heart.) But with Office 365 you can save your files to the cloud and then access them from your other devices.

Also, it can maybe be a much cheaper option for certain programs. I use Microsoft Access and to add that on to a Microsoft 2021 purchase was going to be a couple hundred dollars. But with Office 365 I can have Access along with everything else I need for, at the moment, $8.25 a month. (Go to the business licenses if you need this.)

It also spaces out the cost of the product. You don't have to plunk down all that money on Day 1. But overall Office 365 is probably more expensive for a single user on a single computer than just buying the product with a one-time fee. My laptop that's running Office 2013 is now five years old. If I were paying $8.25 a month I'd have spent $495 which I think is more than I paid up front. And (knock wood) that computer is still going strong.

So it's all about what trade offs you want to make.

To summarize.

There are technically three current versions of Office: (a) the free online one, (b) the static version, the most recent of which is currently Office 2021, and (c) the constantly updating version which is called Office 365.

At the beginner level the differences between the various version should not be significant.

What This Book Covers

Let's talk now about what you will learn in this book, because Excel is an incredibly complex and powerful tool, but it can also get a little overwhelming if you try to cover everything in one go.

So what I've done with the various Excel Essentials series is break that information on Excel down into digestible chunks. And I think I've succeeded at that. (At this point the original *Excel for Beginners* book, which was written for Excel 2013, has over a thousand ratings on Amazon and a rating average of 4.2, so people are generally happy with the level of information covered.)

This book is a version of that book but written for Excel 365. It focuses on the basics of using Excel. We'll cover how to navigate Excel, input data, format it, manipulate it through basic math formulas, filter it, sort it, and print your results.

That should be 95% of what you need to do in Excel day-to-day if you're an average user. I'll also cover at the end how to fill in that last 5% on your own.

(But if you want to keep going with me from there, then there's *Intermediate Excel 365* and *102 Useful Excel 365 Functions* which I'll discuss in a little more detail at the end.)

The other nice thing about Excel is that there are a number of ways to perform the same task. While I do strongly encourage you to learn the control shortcuts (like Ctrl + C to copy) that I mention throughout this book, there will usually be two or three or even more ways to perform a task that we'll cover. So if you have a preference for working in a certain way, it's likely that Excel can accommodate that.

My default is going to be those older ways of doing things because that lets you work across all versions of Excel you may encounter. But when I see that something new works better, I will definitely show that you that method as well.

Okay. So I hope at this point you know that Excel is worth learning.

And I want you to know before we begin that it doesn't have to be hard to learn. Trust me and stick with me through this book and you will have the solid foundation you need.

This book is written to be read start to finish. I want you to read the whole thing. But it's also hopefully organized in such a way that you can come back to it later and use it as a reference for years to come. In the print version there is an index at the end that lists everything we covered and where to find it. (In the ebook version, search will be your friend.)

Now, because this book is about Excel 365, I do need to warn you before we start that Office 365 is a moving target. It is always going to be the latest and greatest. Which means that this book is taking a snapshot of Office 365 as it exists in December 2022, but Office 365 changes monthly.

By the time you read this book, whenever that is, there may be *more* functionality available than I cover here.

Usually, though, that more is not going to impact beginner-level material. For example, the August 2022 update to Excel 365, added a new function (XLOOKUP) and the ability to have "sketched" shapes to make your diagrams and models look hand-drawn, thereby distinguishing ones that were "in progress." Not exactly things that will impact someone new to Excel.

So there will be some changes, but don't worry about them. If I ever think this book isn't a good beginner resource anymore, I will unpublish it or update it. So if you are buying this book new then that means I still think it works for new users and it will still teach you what you need to know to use Excel on a day-to-day basis.

I'm going to be working with the desktop version of Office 365. If you are working online your functionality may be more limited. (That is probably an especially good time to know the control shortcuts.)

Also, your save/open options may be slightly different due to that need to "upload" files or save them to OneDrive.

Okay, one more thing before we get started, which is how to change your appearance, and then we'll dive right in with terminology and absolute basics.

Appearance Settings

Depending on how you have your appearance set, your version of Microsoft Excel may look very different from the screenshots I'm going to use in this book. So before we start I wanted to show you how to change that appearance to match mine in case you want to do that.

If you are absolutely brand new to Excel you may have to come back to this chapter since it relies on having opened an Excel file and knowing some terminology, but I wanted to cover it here before I show you that first screenshot.

To change the appearance of your Office programs, open Excel. That should show you a welcome screen:

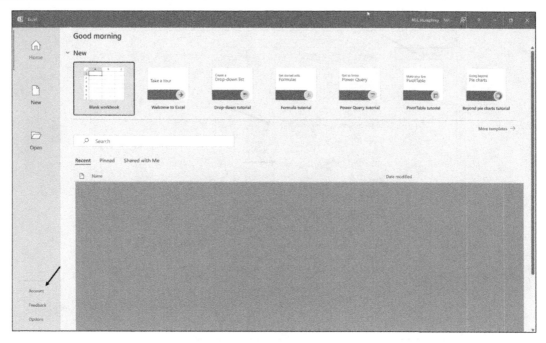

If you don't get that screen, open an Excel file and click on the File option in the top left corner. From there you have two choices. You can either click on Account or Options in the bottom left corner of the screen. Here I've clicked on Account. You can see in the main workspace that there is a dropdown menu for Office Theme. Note that I have mine currently set to Colorful.

If you click on Options instead, then you can find this same setting under Personalize Your Copy of Microsoft Office in the General section:

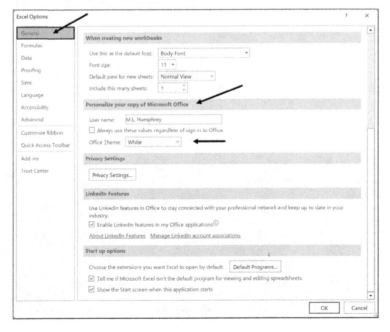

There will be a dropdown menu for Office Theme there as well. Let's look at the different options now.

This is the Dark Gray theme:

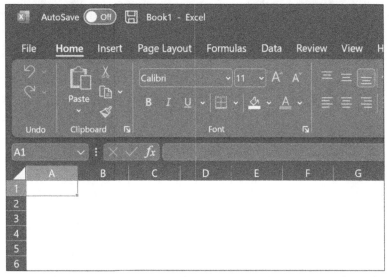

This is the Black theme (which is especially drastic in Word):

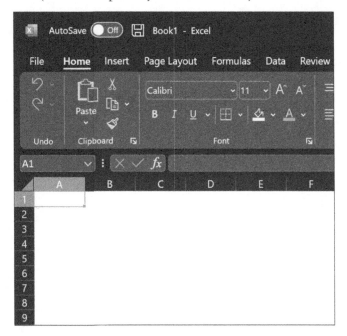

This is the Colorful theme:

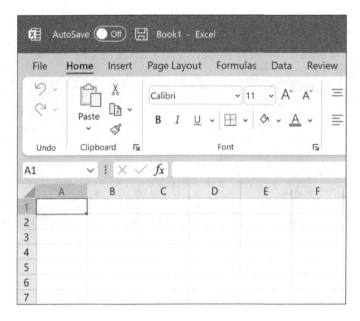

This is the White theme:

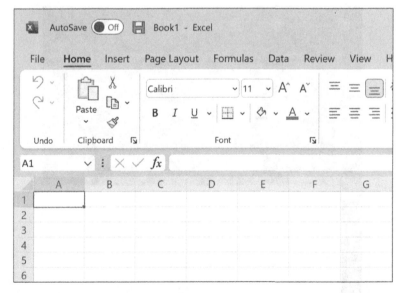

You can't see this in the black and white print version, but the Colorful theme uses blue for the top bar in Word, green for the top bar in Excel, and I would presume orange and red for PowerPoint and Access respectively.

There is also a system settings choice which I presume will be different for everyone based upon the Windows theme they're using. If you have any sort of sight impairment, there are some pretty funky choices you can make in the Windows settings that you may want to explore, but I'm not going to here. One of them for example uses black and bright yellow.

For the rest of this book I'll be using the Colorful theme but it will look just like the White theme most of the time because I won't include the very top of the screen in most of my screenshots.

Whichever choice you make will apply across all of your Office programs, so be careful there. Or be prepared to change it when you move between programs if you have different preferences in different programs.

Okay, now we can cover terminology.

Basic Terminology

Before we can dive in on how to do things, we need to cover some basic terms.

I'm going to assume here you really don't know any of the basics, so you can skim if you think you do, but be sure to at least glance at the headers because I may have my own idiosyncratic way of describing things that you won't have encountered elsewhere.

Workbook

A workbook is what Excel likes to call an Excel file. They define it as a file that contains one or more worksheets. In current versions of Excel a workbook will by default start with one worksheet in it, but you can add more as needed.

Worksheet

Excel defines a worksheet as the primary document you use in Excel to store and work with your data. It can also sometimes be referred to as a spreadsheet, but I will try to avoid using the term spreadsheet here because when I use the term spreadsheet I sometimes actually mean the whole workbook. So better to stick to workbook and worksheet whenever possible.

A worksheet is organized into Columns and Rows that form Cells.

Columns

Excel uses columns and rows to display information. Columns run across the top of the worksheet and, unless you've done something funky with your settings, are identified using letters of the alphabet.

As you can see below, each worksheet will start with A on the far left side for the first column and march right on through the alphabet (A, B, C, D, E, etc.) from there.

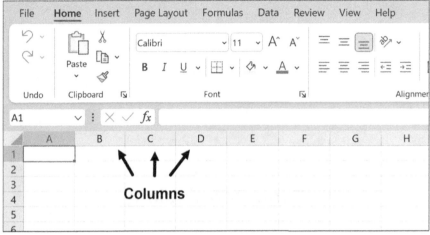

If you scroll far enough to the right, you'll see that the columns continue on to a double alphabet (AA, AB, AC, etc.) and then on to a triple alphabet (AAA, AAB, etc.).

As of right now the very last column in a worksheet is XFD.

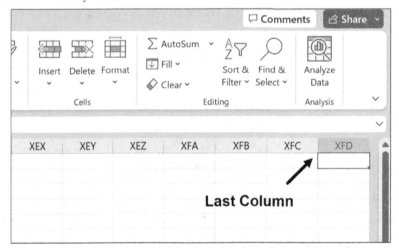

You can reach the very last column in a blank worksheet by holding down the Ctrl key and pressing the End key which is usually also the right arrow key.

If there is already data in that worksheet using Ctrl + End will take you to the last column that has data in it, so you'll need to use Ctrl + End again to go to the last column in the worksheet.

We'll touch on this again, but column letters are basically a way of numbering the columns, not an attribute that is specific to a column. So Column A is always the first column. Column B is always the second column. Etc. And there are always going to be the same number of columns in your worksheet regardless of whether you delete or insert columns.

When you delete or move information in a column you're just moving the data. The grid system doesn't move. So if I take Column A and I delete that column there will still be a Column A because there is still always a first column. And if I were to take all of the data in Column A and move that data three columns over it would now be in Column D.

So think of columns as location information that is actually separate from the data in the worksheet. (We'll work through this more, don't worry.)

Also, columns are one of those areas where you need to be careful if you're working with someone with an older version of Excel because they may not have as many columns in their worksheets in their version of Excel as you do.

For example, I have Excel 2013 on one of my laptops and my last column in that version is IV which means I have far far fewer columns in my version of Excel than anyone using Excel 365 does. This could mean that I would lose data if I open a file from an Excel 365 user in Excel 2013 if that file uses more columns than I have access to.

So always keep in the back of your mind that if you're working with others that aren't set up the same way you are in Office that you can have compatibility issues and one of the main ones you can have is number of rows and columns.

But let's get back to basic terms.

Rows

Rows run down the side of each worksheet and are numbered starting at 1 and up to a very high number. As of now that number is 1048576. That means a single Excel worksheet currently has over a million rows. You can hold down the Ctrl key in a blank worksheet while hitting the down arrow to see just how many rows your version of Excel has.

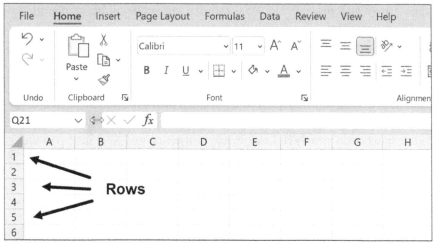

As a comparison, Excel 2013 had only 65,536 rows in a worksheet. Keep this in mind for compatibility issues when working with other users.

And, once more, those row numbers are locational information. The first row will always be numbered 1. The second row will always be numbered 2. And so on and so forth. And at least as of this moment there will always be 1,048,576 rows in every Excel worksheet at all times. So even if you delete or insert rows that will not change that fact.

You are deleting data not the number of rows in the worksheet.

Cells

Cells are where the row and column data all comes together. Think of it as map coordinates. Cell A1 is the first column and first row of the worksheet.

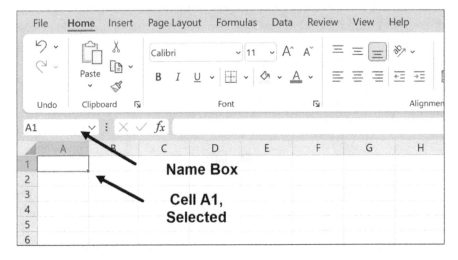

When you click onto a specific cell, like I have above, that cell will be surrounded with a darker border around the perimeter.

You can also look in the Name Box, noted above, to see the cell reference for that cell. These cell references are used when writing Excel formulas or using functions.

And remember, that these are coordinates, they are not fixed to your data. So if you have an entry in the first column of the first row of your worksheet and move that entry to the third column and third row of your worksheet that entry will now be in Cell C3 not Cell A1.

(Again, don't worry too much right now, we will work in Excel and you will see how this happens.)

Click

If I tell you to click on something, that means to use your mouse (or trackpad) to move the cursor on the screen over to a specific location and left-click or right-click on the option. (See the next definition for the difference between left-click and right-click).

If you left-click, this selects the item. If you right-click, this generally displays a dropdown list of options to choose from. If I don't tell you which to do, left- or right-click, then left-click.

Left-click/Right-click

If you look at your mouse you generally have two flat buttons to press. One is on the left side, one is on the right.

If I say left-click that means to press down on the button on the left. If I say right-click that means press down on the button on the right. (If you're used to using Word you may already do this without even thinking about it. So, if that's the case then think of left-click as what you usually use to select text and right-click as what you use to see a menu of choices.)

If you're using a track pad, not all track pads have the left- and right-hand areas visible. In that case, you'll basically want to press on either the bottom left-hand side of the track pad or the bottom right-hand side of the trackpad as needed.

Select

If I tell you to "select" cells, that means to highlight them. If the cells are next to each other, you can just left-click on the first one and drag the cursor (move your mouse or finger on the trackpad) as you hold that left-click until all of the cells are highlighted.

(I will refer to this action as left-click and drag.)

When you do this, all the selected cells will be shaded gray and surrounded by a dark box like below except for the first cell you clicked on which will be within the perimeter of the box but will be white.

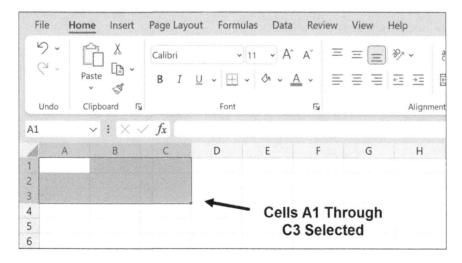

Cells A1 Through
C3 Selected

You can also select cells that are not next to each other by holding down the Ctrl key as you left-click on each cell.

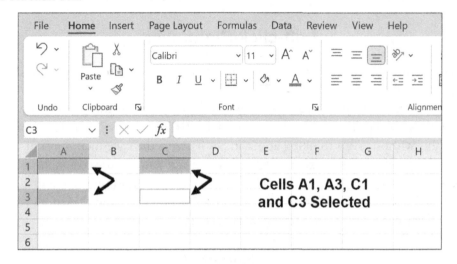

When you do that, each selected cell will be shaded gray except for the last selected cell which will be surrounded by a border but will be white. Above I selected Cells A1, A3, C1, and C3. C3 was selected last.

To select an entire column, click on the letter. To select an entire row, click on the number.

For any row or column where a cell is selected in that row or column, the number or letter for that row or column will be shaded differently. In my version right now with my settings it's shaded a darker gray and the number/letter turns green.

For any row or column where the whole row or column is selected that letter or number will change to a different shading. For my version with my settings it turns light green with a dark green number/letter.

Data

Data is the information you enter into your worksheet. It's the values and text that you input or calculate. I will also sometimes refer to this as information, values, or text.

Data Table

I may also sometimes refer to a data table or table of data. This is just a combination of cells that contain data in them.

One thing to keep in mind with Excel versus Word if you're coming from using Word is that in Word when you create a data table you are adding a specific number of rows and columns into Word to do that. But in Excel the number of rows and columns never changes.

What does change is how many of those rows or columns have your data in them.

Excel is smart enough to only print or focus on the rows or columns with data in them, but if you want something to print out and look like a table you could create in Word you'll want to put borders around your data in Excel. (We'll discuss how to do that, don't worry.)

(This is a question that came up a few times after I released *Excel for Beginners*, so I wanted to mention it here specifically. Data tables as you create them in Word are not the same as data tables as you use them in Excel.)

Arrow

I will sometimes tell you to arrow to somewhere. Or to arrow right, left, up, or down. This just means to use the arrow keys. Using arrows is one way to move between cells within an Excel worksheet.

The other ways are to left-click on a cell. Or you can use Tab and Shift + Tab to move right and left, respectively. And Enter to move to the next row.

Cursor Functions

The cursor is what moves around when you move your mouse or use the trackpad. In Excel the cursor changes its appearance depending on what functions you can perform. You can see this by opening an Excel file and moving your cursor over the cells and then along the edges of a row or column and then up to the menu options up top.

Tab

I am going to talk a lot about Tabs, which are the options you have to choose from at the top of the workspace.

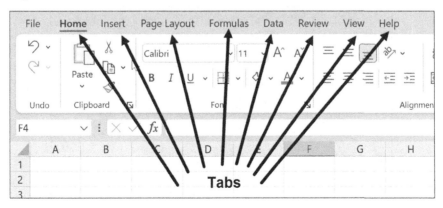

It used to be, in older versions of Excel that when you clicked on one of these options it took on the appearance of a tab like a file folder has. But in the latest versions of Excel that's no longer the case. The selected tab is just underlined. For example, in the image above, I have the Home tab selected which you can tell from the solid line under the word Home.

Each tab has a number of options available. Here is the left-hand set of options available under the Home tab, for example:

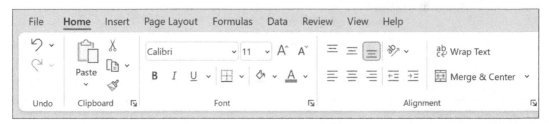

I can Undo, Copy/Paste/Format Sweep, choose my font attributes, choose my text alignment, etc.

The Home tab is the tab that will be selected by default. But you can click on the other tabs to see their available options.

Throughout this book I will often tell you to go to Y section of X tab and choose the task that we're trying to complete. For example, if I wanted you to change the font from Calibri to something else, I would say you could go to the Font section of the Home tab and click on the dropdown menu for font. (I will include screenshots most of the time so you can also see what I'm talking about.)

Dropdown Menus

A dropdown menu is a listing of available choices that you can see when you click on the arrow for that option or right-click in certain places such as the main workspace.

For example, here is the font dropdown menu:

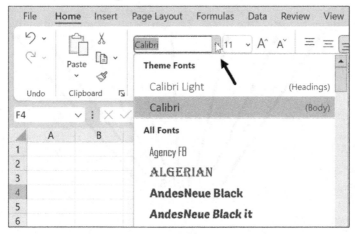

I clicked on the small arrow next to the current font name and that brought up a listing of choices. There are a large number of dropdown menus in Excel as you can see here where we have dropdown menus for Undo, Paste, Copy, Font, Font Size, Underline, Borders, Fill Color, Font Color, and Text Orientation:

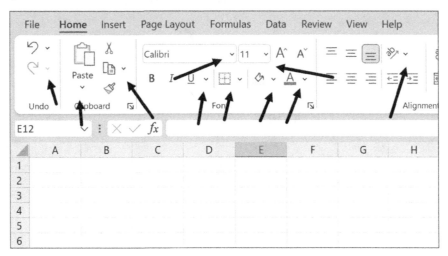

There are many more available in Excel. So any time I tell you to use a dropdown menu or anytime you're trying to find additional options, look for that little arrow to the right of or below the task you're trying to complete or try right-clicking on a worksheet name or in the main workspace.

Help Text

This isn't really a term and we'll discuss it again later, but I just wanted to mention that if you are ever unsure what task an image in the top menu is related to, you can usually hold your mouse over the image and Excel will tell you what it is. Here, for example, I held my cursor over the image of a bucket with a bright yellow line under it and Excel showed me a pop-up box that tells me that's for adding Fill Color and what that does. I can then click on Tell Me More to open Help and learn more about how it works.

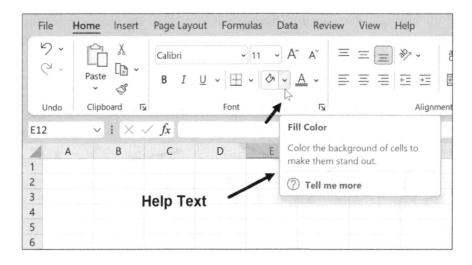

Tell Me More is not always available, but usually you will at least get a brief description of what that image will let you do.

Dialogue Boxes

Dialogue boxes are pop-up boxes that contain additional choices. You will often see one if you click on the arrow in the corner of a section of a tab. For example, here I have clicked on the arrow in the corner of the Font section of the Home tab and that has opened the Format Cells dialogue box.

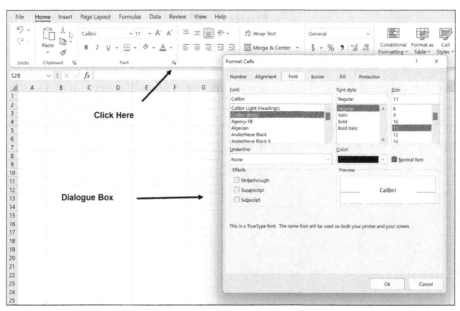

Dialogue boxes often have the most available choices. So if you aren't seeing what you want in the tab choices, then click on that arrow to open the related dialogue box if it exists.

Also, for those who are used to older versions of Excel, dialogue boxes are likely what you're used to working with so using them can sometimes feel more familiar than using the options up top.

You will also sometimes see a dialogue box if you right-click and choose an option from the dropdown menu in the main workspace.

Scroll Bars

When you have more information than will show on the screen, dialogue box, or dropdown menu you can use the scroll bars to see the rest of the information.

The main scroll bars you will see are going to be in the main workspace when there is more data in your rows and columns than can appear on the screen:

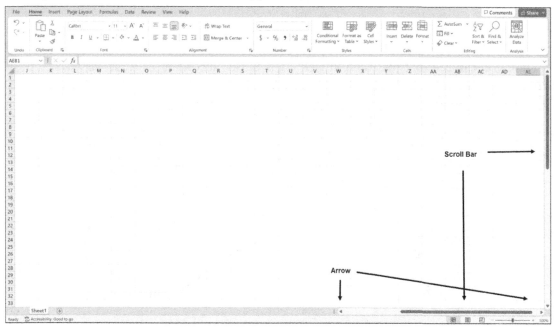

Scroll bars usually appear on the right-hand side or on the bottom of the workspace, dialogue box, or dropdown menu.

In the image above you can see them as darker gray bars. Note that there are also arrows at each end of the scroll bars. And that there is blank space between the arrows and those bars.

The more information involved, the smaller the scroll bars will be and the more space there will be around them.

There are three ways to navigate using the scroll bars.

You can left- click and drag the bar itself. This means, left-click on the bar, hold down the left-click, and move the cursor as you do so. The bar will move and the visible information will change.

If you only want to move a small amount at a time, you can use the arrows. Arrows at the bottom will move one item left or right, arrows on the side will move one item up or down.

You can also, left-click and hold on the arrows to move through multiple items but it will do so one at a time.

The final option is to click into the gray space between the two. One click in that gray space will move you an entire screen's worth. So in the main workspace if I can see Columns A through V and I click in the gray space at the bottom that moves me to Columns W through AR.

In the main workspace, you can only use the scroll bars or click into that gray space to navigate within the area where you have data. But the arrows will let you go past that.

Formula Bar

The formula bar is the long white bar at the top of the main workspace directly below the menu tabs that lets you see the actual contents of a cell, not just the display value.

Here you can see that the value in Cell C1 is 5, but according to what we can see in the formula bar, that value is calculated using the formula =A1+B1, which adds the values in Cells A1 and B1 together:

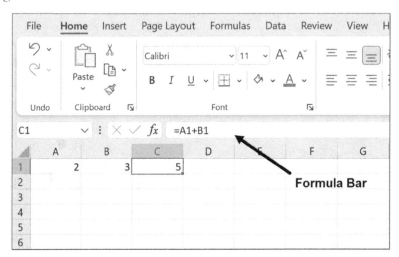

Task Pane

On occasion Excel will open a task pane, which is different from a dialogue box because it is part of the workspace. You can use F1 to see an example of this with the Help task pane which opens on the right-hand side of the workspace.

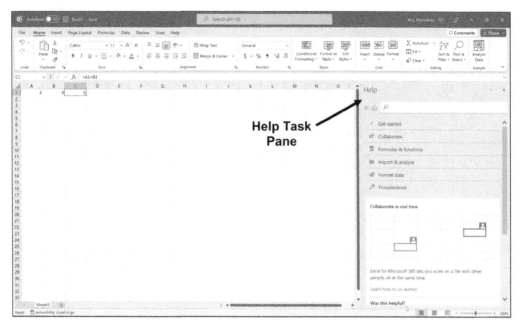

They can be closed by clicking on the X in the top right corner.

Absolute Basics

Before we start working in an Excel workbook, I want to cover the absolute basics of opening, saving, closing, and deleting files.

If you're already familiar with Microsoft Word or another Office program or similar, then this will probably all be familiar to you, but I want to make sure it's here for those who aren't.

Open a New Excel File

If you want to start a brand new Excel file, the first step is to open Excel. How you do this will depend on how you have your computer set up and what version of Windows you're running.

One of the first things I do when I get a new computer is I add my key programs to my taskbar. That way when I want to open Excel I can just click on the icon for Excel and open the program.

In Windows 11, a simple click on that green icon with the X will open Excel.

If you aren't set up with that, then you may have an Excel shortcut on your desktop.

Or you can go to the Start menu in the bottom left corner of your computer (if you haven't moved things around), left-click on that blue window icon and it will show you a menu where Excel may be in your pinned apps. If it's not there you can search for it. Or you can go to All Apps and find it there.

This is Windows 11. Windows 10, you click on the Start menu icon and look for the All Apps listing and then find it that way. They'll probably change it again in Windows 12 or whatever comes next, because they seem to love to do that, which is why I find it once, right-click, and choose to Pin to Taskbar so it's right there when I need it.

Okay. So however you do it, open Excel. If this is your first time in Excel you may have to Activate your account or skip through some screens that want you to activate it. But after you do that, you'll have something like this:

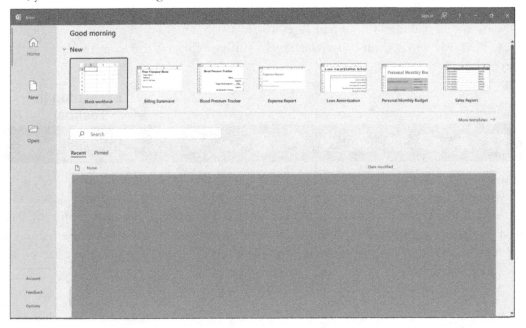

This is the Excel welcome screen. I've grayed out the section with my recent files listed, but otherwise this is what you should see when you first open Excel.

Those appearance settings we talked about before can be changed using Options on the left-hand side, bottom corner.

But if you're there to start a new file, then click on the Blank Workbook choice at the top of the screen.

(You'll see that there are also a number of templates you can choose from, but for what we're going to do in this book you can ignore those for now. If at some point you want to create an expense report, for example, you may want to click on that template and adjust from there.)

You could also click on New on the left-hand side but that just takes you to another screen where you have the Blank Workbook and template choices once more.

Clicking on Blank Workbook will open a new, blank workbook for you that looks like this:

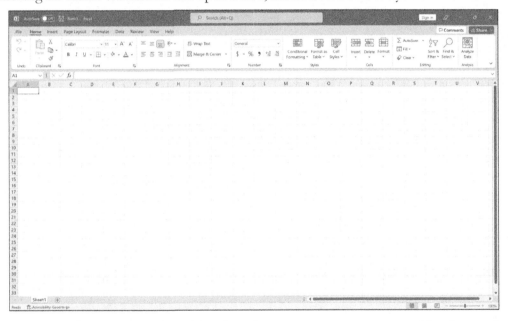

If you are already in an Excel workbook and want to create a new workbook, you have a couple of choices. The easiest is to use Ctrl + N. That will immediately create a new workbook for you.

You can also go to the top of the screen, click on the File option, and then click on Blank Workbook from there.

Open An Existing Excel File

If you already have an Excel file and now want to open that file and work on it, there are a couple of options available.

The first is to find the Excel file wherever you have it saved and double-click on it. That will open the file in Excel and if Excel isn't already open will also open Excel for you.

If you do have Excel open and you've recently used that file, then you should be able to find it in your Recent Files listing on the welcome screen when you open Excel.

You can see in the image below the four most recent files I've opened in Excel and when they were opened last. My screen actually shows eight files and if I scroll down there are two more for a total of ten.

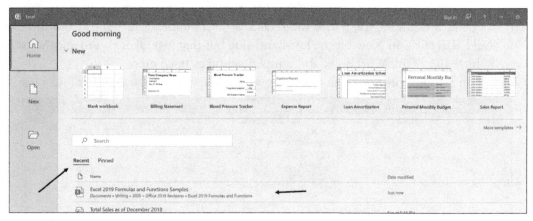

Click on the file name and the file will open.

There may be times when a file is listed in your recent files list but you can't open it from there. This happens if you move the file or change its name outside of Excel.

For a file that you want to open that isn't in that recent files list, click on Open from the welcome screen. You will once more see the Recent Files listing, but there will also be other options. One of those is the Folders option. Click on that and you'll see a listing of any folders that contain files you recently opened.

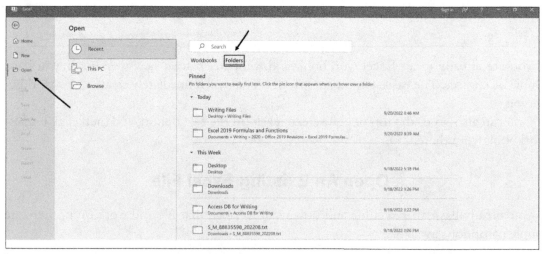

You can see in the image above that I opened files from the Writing Files and Excel 2019 Formulas and Functions folders today and have opened files from my Desktop, Downloads, Access DB for Writing, and a zip file this week.

This can sometimes be the easiest way to find a file you're looking for if you tend to store your Excel files in just a handful of locations. Click on one of those folder options and you'll see a listing of Excel files that are in that folder. You can then click on that file name to open it.

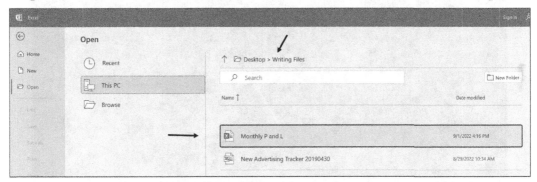

That will often be the best way to find a file. But it doesn't work if the folder the file is in is one you haven't used recently. It also doesn't work if the file you want to open isn't one of the main types of files that Excel can open, namely, .xls, .xlsx, or .csv.

If that's the case, then click on the Browse option instead. This will open the Open dialogue box.

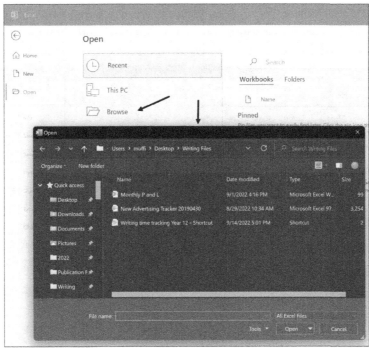

You can then use the options on the left-hand side to navigate to the folder that contains your file and select the file that way.

One of the files I need to open in Excel is a .txt file. By default, Excel will not look for that file type. You can see here that it's not showing any files for me to open.

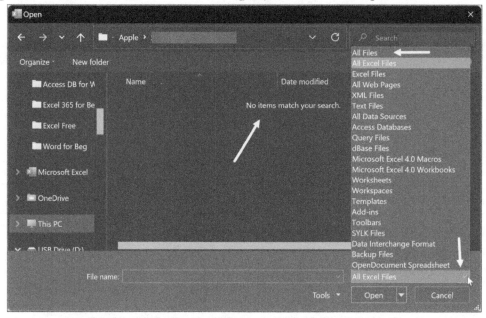

When I need to open one of those Text files, I have to change the file type in the Open dialogue box by clicking on the dropdown menu for file type and changing it to All Files from All Excel Files. Once I do that, I can then see the file I need to open and select that file:

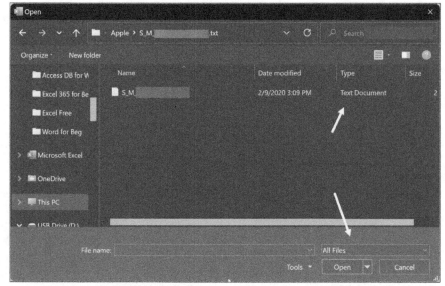

But that's a pretty rare situation, so usually you won't need to worry about that. I just mention it here because for anyone who publishes through Apple, their reports are text files. (That you also have to open with 7-Zip.)

Okay, back to things that matter to most readers instead of just one little subset.

If you already have Excel open and are either working on a file already or are in that main workspace and want to open another file, you can either use Ctrl + O, which will take you to the Open screen, or you can click on File at the top of the workspace and then click on Open.

From there it's the same steps as we just walked through.

Pin A File

If you have a file that you always want readily accessible but that won't stay in your recent files listing because you open enough files that it sometimes falls out of your top ten most recent, then you can Pin that file and it will always be available to you in your Pinned files section.

For example, I have a monthly profit and loss Excel file that I like to review once a month. But it gets lost from my recent files list because when I load all of my sales reports there are more than ten of them. So to make sure I can always find that file, I pin it.

To do this, find the file in your recent files list. Hold your cursor over that listing. You should see the image of a thumbtack appear on the right-hand side, and if you hold your cursor over that image it will say, "Pin this item to the list".

Click on that thumbtack. If you then click onto the Pinned option, that file will be listed there. And it will stay there regardless of what other files you open, so that it's always available to you.

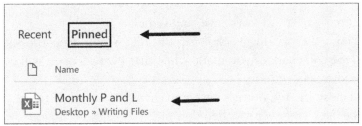

Once you've pinned a file, you can open it by going to your Pinned Files section and clicking on that name.

Close a File

If you ever have an Excel file open and want to close it, you can use Ctrl + W. I personally never remember that particular shortcut, so I instead just click on the X in the top right-hand corner.

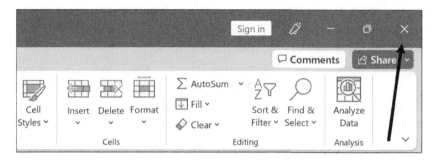

You can also click on File in the top menu on the right-hand side and then click on Close from the list of options on the left-hand side of the File screen.

Save a File

If you've made changes to a file and you try to close it Excel will show you a dialogue box that asks if you want to save those changes.

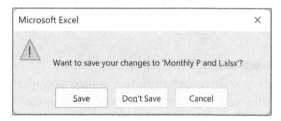

It gives you three options, Save, Don't Save, and Cancel.

Save will overwrite the existing version of the file. You'll keep the same file name, file location, and file type. All changes you made while that file was open will be saved. Whatever the file was like before that, is gone.

Don't Save will close the file but not save any changes you made to the document while it was open. It will be like you never touched that file.

Cancel will not close the file and also not save the changes. Choose Cancel if you want to save the file as a new version and not overwrite the old version.

If you're trying to close a brand new file, choosing Save will actually open the Save As dialogue box, because Excel doesn't know where you want to save the file or what you want to call it.

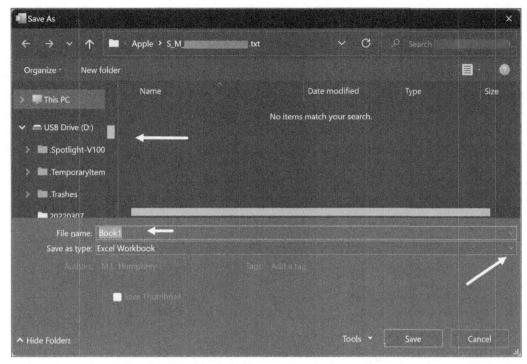

It will default to wherever the last file you opened was saved and the name will be some variation on Book 1. (If you have multiple blank workbooks opened it may be Book 2 or Book 3, etc.)

Type in the new name you want. Use the folders on the left-hand side of the dialogue box to navigate to the folder where you want to save that file. And make sure that the file type is what you want to use. Normally you'll be fine sticking with a file type of Excel Workbook.

But file type is another area where you may run into issues if someone is using an older version of Excel than you are. In that case, change the file type to Excel 97-2003 Workbook.

Be careful doing this, though, because as Excel adds more and more bells and whistles and functionality it makes it more and more likely that the Excel 97-2003 file format is not going to be able to support something you did in your Excel file.

If you're ever looking at file extensions, this is the difference between a .xlsx file and a .xls file. All files before Excel 2007 were .xls files. All files since then are .xlsx. In the past I advised saving to .xls for compatibility reasons, but I think we're far enough along at this point with .xlsx that you don't need to do that by default anymore. And if you're only working on files for yourself or your organization, you absolutely shouldn't need to worry about that.

If that all sounded confusing, don't worry. Just save as Excel Workbook. And if someone ever says, "I can't open that file because I have an older version of Excel," then come back to this section at that point in time.

So that's how you save a file if you weren't being proactive about it and just waited for Excel to remind you to save your file before you closed it.

But it's possible you will want to save that file under a new name or in a new location or as a new file type. Or that you'll want to save as you work so that if your computer crashes you don't lose your work. (Not as much of an issue these days as it was in the past, but it can still happen.)

In that case, let's start with Save first. Save is for a file where you want to save the changes you've made but you don't need to change the name, location, or file type.

The easiest option is Ctrl + S. That will save all of the changes you've made so far and overwrite the former version of the file.

If the file has never been saved before it will take you to the Save As screen under the File tab.

You can also click on the computer disk icon in the top left corner of the screen. Hold your mouse over it and it will say Save (Ctrl + S). Click on that and that too will save any changes you've made so far and overwrite the existing file.

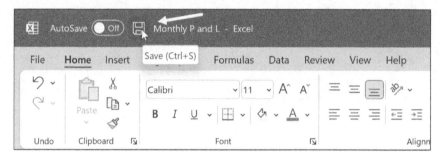

To save the file you're working on under a new name, into a new location, or as a new file type, you need to use Save As. To do that, click on File in the top left corner and then choose Save As.

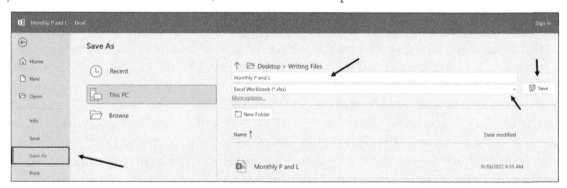

If you just need to change the file name, you can do so right there. Same with the file type. Once done click on Save.

To change the location, click on the Browse option. That will bring up the Save As dialogue box and let you navigate to the new location you want. Clicking on More Options will also bring up that dialogue box.

Keep in mind with Save As that the original file will still exist. So if you want multiple versions of a file, which I sometimes do when I'm building something really complex, that's great. But if what you really wanted was to change the file name or move the file, then you probably don't want to use Save As to do that.

Change a File Name

To change the name of an Excel file you can use Save As as we just discussed but that will leave you with two files. The original file will have the original name and then the newly-saved version will have the new name.

But if you don't need two files, it's better to close the Excel file, go directly to the folder where you have the file saved and change the name there. To do so, click on the file once to select it, and then click on it a second to make the name editable.

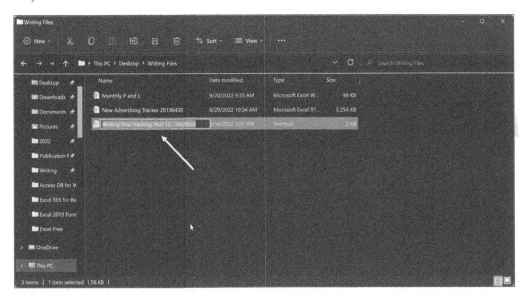

You can see here that I've done that with the third listed file so that the text of the name is now highlighted. I can then click into that field and make whatever change I want to the name. When you're done, hit Enter.

If you change a file name in this way, you will not be able to use the Recent or Pinned file listing to open the file the next time you go to open it in Excel. You will have to open the file directly from where it's saved or use the Browse option.

Delete a File

If you ever want to permanently delete an Excel file. Say, for example, that you did use Save

As but don't need that original file anymore, this has to be done outside of Excel. Close the file in Excel and then go find where you have it saved. Click on the file name once to select it. And then click on the trash can icon at the top of the window. You can also right-click on the file name and click on the trash can from there (for Windows 11) or choose Delete from the dropdown menu (for Windows 10).

File Naming Tip

Before we close out this chapter, I just want to share a file-naming tip I picked up from an efficiency training years ago that's been very helpful for me. I do keep multiple versions of files. For example, when I publish a book there's the original file. And then if I later make an edit because I find a typo or I release a new book in that series that needs to be added to the Also By section, there's another file. Some of my titles have twenty versions because they've been out almost a decade by now.

I want those files to display in an order that lets me quickly find the most recent one. To make that happen, I use a YYYYMMDD naming format.

This book for example would be "Excel 365 for Beginners 20221210". And then if I made an edit on December 15th it would be "Excel 365 for Beginners 20221215". By writing the date in that order–year, month, day–it ensures that when I sort by name, the files sort in proper date order.

(And if I ever for some reason have two on the same day then I add v1, v2, etc. at the end.)

You can use this same trick for folder names as well.

Also, if you have a process that involves multiple files and steps, consider how things will sort there as well. For example, I have put some of my books out as audiobooks. And there are four steps I go through to get to the final file. I have the raw recording, the first pass edit, the Reaper processing, and then the final version. I want to keep all of the raw files together, all the first pass files together, etc. And I want them in order.

So in that case I name the files "Raw 1 Introduction", "First Pass 1 Introduction", etc. By putting the stage of production first that makes sure that the raw files for all fifteen chapters group together. And by using the chapter number next I make sure that the first file in each group is the first chapter.

You will save yourself a lot of headache if you give some thought to your file names up front. And if you don't do so, well, you can always go and rename those files later. Just remember to do it where you saved the files not through Excel.

Okay. Now that we know how to open, close, save, rename, and delete files, let's talk about how to navigate Excel.

Navigating Excel

I want to talk now about how to move around within an Excel worksheet as well as within an Excel workbook and between workbooks.

Move Between Excel Workbooks

Let's start with the easiest one. If you have two Excel workbooks open, the easiest way to move between them is using Alt + Tab. If you have more than two files open just keeping using the Tab key while you hold down the Alt key to cycle through until you reach the one you want.

Alt + Tab lets you cycle through all of your open files or programs, not just Excel.

Items will usually be listed in order of when you last used them, so if you're moving back and forth between two Excel files, even if you have ten items open, those two files should be your first option each time you move. That means just one use of Alt + Tab will take you to the other file.

Another option, is to hold your mouse over the icon for Excel in the taskbar and then choose the file you want that way by clicking on the thumbnail image for the file.

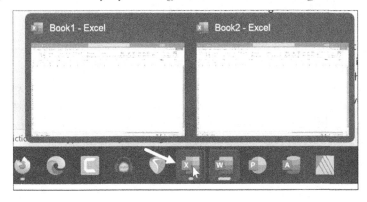

Move Between Excel Worksheets

Within an Excel file it is possible to have multiple Excel worksheets. I usually just click on the name of the worksheet I want at the bottom of the workspace.

You can see which worksheet you are currently on by seeing which worksheet name is white with bolded text.

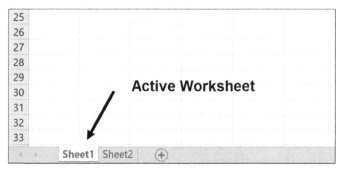

There is also a control shortcut for moving between worksheets that I generally don't use. Ctrl + Page Up will move you one worksheet to the left and Ctrl + Page Down will move you one worksheet to the right. If like on my computer your Page Up and Page Down buttons are combined with your up and down arrows then you may need to use Ctrl + Fn + Page Up and Ctrl + Fn + Page Down.

This does not, as of this moment, cycle through to the start or to the end. Meaning, if you have twenty worksheets and want to get from the first to the last, you would have to use Ctrl + Page Down nineteen times. Just using Ctrl + Page Up isn't an option. (It would be nice if it was, though, so maybe they'll do that someday.)

If you have more worksheets in your file than can be displayed at the bottom of the workspace, there will be little … at the end of the visible worksheet names.

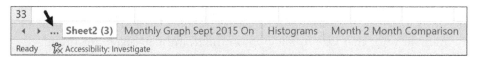

Click on that … to see more worksheets. You can also use those left and right arrows on the bottom left corner of the workspace to move left or right and show more worksheets.

Using Ctrl and left-clicking on one of those two arrows will take you all the way to the first sheet or all the way to the last sheet, depending on which arrow you click on.

You can also right-click on one of those arrows to bring up an Activate dialogue box listing all of your worksheets in your workbook. From there click on the name of the worksheet you want and then click on OK and Excel will take you to that worksheet.

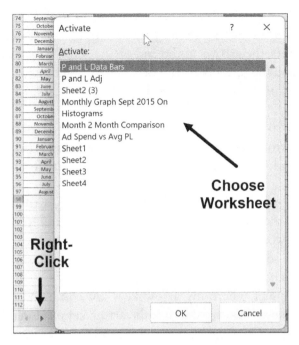

(If you don't want to try to remember those last two, holding your mouse over the arrows will tell you that as well. When in doubt in Excel, try holding the cursor over something because often there will be additional help text that appears.)

Move Within An Excel Worksheet

Any brand new Excel workbook is going to open on Sheet 1 and in Cell A1. To move from there, as we discussed briefly in the terminology section, you have a few options.

You can simply use the arrow keys to move one cell in any direction. So, right arrow moves you right one cell to Cell B1. Or if you used the down arrow it would move you down one cell to Cell A2. And then once you're not pinned into a corner in Cell A1, you can also use the left arrow to go left one cell and the up arrow to go up one cell.

The Tab key will also let you go right one cell. And using Shift and the Tab key will let you go left one cell.

Enter will also move you down one cell. Although, sometimes if you're entering data Enter will actually move you down one row but over to the beginning of where you were entering your data. So, for example, if I put "a" in Cell A1, "b" in Cell B1, and "c" in Cell C1, and then hit Enter that will take me to Cell A2. This can be very useful when entering multiple rows and columns of data directly into Excel.

Page Up and Page Down will take you one full screen's worth of rows up or down. (You may need to use Fn + Page Up and Fn + Page Down depending on how your computer is set up.)

You can also simply left-click into whichever cell you want if it's visible in your workspace.

As discussed more fully in the terminology section, to move greater distances within a file, you can use the scroll bars, the arrows at the end of the scroll bars, or click on the gray space between those arrows and the scroll bars. But be careful using those, because what you see will adjust, but until you click into a cell in the worksheet, you will still be in the last cell you were clicked into or edited.

This has occasionally tripped me up when I have my panes frozen (something we'll talk about later) and then I scroll far down in my data, but forget to click into one of the cells I can see on the workspace and so hit enter and am suddenly back at Row 2 instead of Row 2,354 or whatever.

Also, as mentioned before, according to Microsoft's help, Ctrl + End and Ctrl + Page Down will move you to the end of a range of data or the end of your worksheet, depending on if there's data in the worksheet.

Likewise, to go from somewhere in your worksheet to the top or the left-most edge, you can use Ctrl + Page Up and Ctrl + Home.

For me, with a computer where my arrow keys are combined with my Page Up, Page Down, Home and End keys I just have to use the arrow keys. I don't need to add the Fn key in to this one to get to Page Up, Page Down, Home, and End. So you may need to experiment around a bit to see how your particular computer acts.

Also, the help text on this one seems to differ from how it actually works. The help text says it takes you to the outer range of any existing data, but from testing it, what it actually does is takes you to the end of the next set of data in that particular row or column.

So if Column A has data for six rows and Column B has data for ten rows, depending on which column you're in when you use the shortcut you may go six rows or you may go ten.

If you do use this, and it can be very handy especially when paired with Shift so that you select those cells at the same time, watch out for gaps in your data. If there is an empty column or an empty row, Excel will stop at that gap. You'll need to use the arrow/page up/page down/home/end key again to grab the full range of your data if that happens.

Freeze Panes

If you have a lot of information in a worksheet, Freeze Panes will save you. Because it lets you keep certain information, such as a header row, visible in your workspace while you scroll down to see more data. Without freeze panes you end up with a screen full of data but nothing that tells you what that data is.

Here, for example, is a few rows of data from one of my Amazon reports:

	A	C	E	F	G	H	I	J	K	L
68	2021-01-26	Author A	Amazon.com		70% Standard	1	0	1	4.99	4.99
69	2021-01-26	Author F	Amazon.com		35% Free - Price Match	1	0	1	0.99	0.00
70	2021-01-26	Author A	Amazon.com		70% Standard	2	0	2	4.99	4.99
71	2021-01-26	Author D	Amazon.com		70% Standard	1	0	1	3.99	3.99
72	2021-01-25	Author A	Amazon.com		70% Standard	3	0	3	4.99	4.99
73	2021-01-25	Author B	Amazon.co.uk		70% Standard	1	0	1	3.99	3.99
74	2021-01-25	Author A	Amazon.com		70% Standard	1	0	1	2.99	2.99
75	2021-01-25	Author B	Amazon.com		70% Standard	1	0	1	4.99	4.99

If you wanted to use one of those columns to know the total number of units sold, which one would you use? And which one would show list price of the book? Versus which one shows what a customer actually paid for the book? Some of it is self-explanatory, but not all of it.

This particular report also has 15 columns, which means that I either would need to Zoom Out and make the text smaller to see everything or I'm going to not be able to see the left-most columns when I'm looking at the right-most column.

Which is a problem. I have it hidden right now, but Column B is Title and looking at how much I earned in the second-to-last column doesn't do me much good if I don't know which book it is.

But Freeze Panes lets me solve this issue. Because I can set up this worksheet so that Row 1 is always visible even when I'm on Row 250. And I can also set it up so that my title column is always visible, too.

Like so:

	A	B	N	O	P
1	**Royalty Date**	**Title**	**Royalty**	**Currency**	
224	2021-01-06	Book Title	2.76	USD	
225	2021-01-06	Book Title	3.96	USD	
226	2021-01-06	Book Title	2.05	USD	
227	2021-01-06	Book Title	5.90	USD	
228	2021-01-06	Book Title	2.76	USD	
229	2021-01-06	Book Title	5.83	USD	
230	2021-01-06	Book Title	2.76	USD	

See how it goes from Row 1 to Row 224? And how it shows Columns A and B and then Columns N and O? All of the other rows and columns are still visible, but I've scrolled down and over to see this information.

So how do you set this up?

If all you want is to freeze the top row of your worksheet or the first column, go to the Window section of the View tab and click on the dropdown arrow for Freeze Panes. Choose either Freeze Top Row or Freeze First Column.

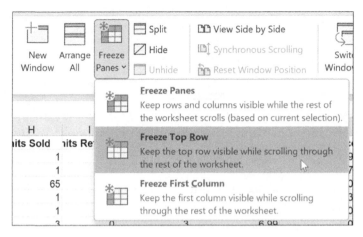

You can do one or the other this way, but not both. If you want to freeze more than one column, more than one row, or columns and rows both at the same time, then you need to first click into your worksheet at the first cell that you are okay *not* seeing.

In other words, below the rows that you want to freeze in place and to the right of the columns that you want to freeze in place.

So in our example worksheet, I want to keep the first row visible and I want book title visible, which is in the second column. That means I need to click into Cell C2.

	A	B	C	E	F
1	Royalty Date	Title	Author Name	Marketplace	Royalty Type
2	2021-01-31	Book Title	Author A	Amazon.com	70%
3	2021-01-31	Book Title	Author B	Amazon.com.au	70%
4	2021-01-31	Book Title	Author C	Amazon.com	70%
5	2021-01-31	Book Title	Author D	Amazon.com	70%
6	2021-01-31	Book Title	Author C	Amazon.fr	70%
7	2021-01-31	Book Title	Author C	Amazon.ca	70%

In the image above you can see that I've shaded the first row gray as well as the two columns on the left gray so that I can make it more clear which data will remain visible.

I can then go to the Freeze Panes dropdown and choose the first option, Freeze Panes, to keep both that top row and the left two columns visible.

Now, honestly I don't care about keeping the date visible, but with freeze panes you don't get to be that specific. So it's everything to the left and everything above the cell you choose. Which means if I want book title I am also going to get date.

(I could hide a column or move a column to fix that, but it's not that big a deal to me.)

To remove freeze panes, just go back to that same dropdown menu. The top option will be Unfreeze Panes now and you can just click on it to remove any freeze panes that are in effect.

Now, one thing to be careful of, that I do more than I should. If you are clicked into Row 1 and have freeze panes in effect and have scrolled down to Row 10,522 but not clicked into any cell in that row or in that part of your data, you are still on Row 1 as far as Excel is concerned. And so if you use your down arrow you will go to Row 2 and the rows you see on your workspace will change to Rows 2 through…37 or so. And then you'll have to scroll all the way back down to Row 10,522 again.

Also, don't try to freeze too many rows or columns at a time. If you freeze the majority of your screen then you'll only be able to scroll maybe one record at a time which is very inefficient.

Hide Columns or Rows

Sometimes when I'm working with data in Excel there will be rows of data or columns of data I really don't need to see at all. So it's not that there's so much information on the screen I can't see it all, it's more that I want what's in Column B next to what's in Column F. Maybe I'm inputting data into those two columns, but there are calculations between the two that I want to stay where they are. So while I'm adding my information I don't need to see the calculation columns, just the columns where I'm putting in information.

When that happens I hide those rows or columns I don't need to see.

To hide a row or column, right-click on the letter or number for that column or row, and choose Hide from the dropdown menu.

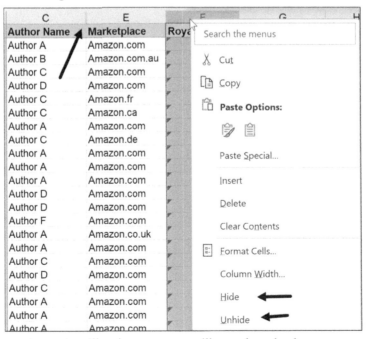

When you hide a column it still exists, so you will see that the letters or numbers skip that missing column or row. It will go from Column C to Column E, for example, if you've hidden Column D like I have in the screenshot above.

To unhide hidden columns or rows, select the columns or rows on either side of the hidden entries and then right-click and choose Unhide.

* * *

Now let's talk about inputting data after which we'll talk about inserting and deleting rows, columns, and cells as well as a bit more about working with worksheets.

Input Data

At its most basic, inputting your data is very simple. Click in the cell where you want to input information and then type. But there are some tricks to it that you'll want to keep in mind.

First, let's take a step back and talk about one of the key strengths of using Excel and that's the ability to sort or filter your data.

For example, I publish books and every month I get reports from the places where my books are published listing all of the sales of my books at those locations.

But what if I only care about the sales of book A? How can I see those if I have a couple hundred rows of information in the report they've given me?

Well, if the site where I sold those books is nice and helpful and they understand data analysis, they've given me my sales listings in an Excel worksheet with one header row at the top and then one row for each sale or for each book.

If they've done that, then I can very easily filter my data on the title column and see just the entries related to title A. Or create a pivot table of that data so I can see all sales for that title grouped together.

If they haven't, then I'm stuck deleting rows of information I don't need to get to the data I want.

Which is all a roundabout way of saying that you can input your data any way you want, but if you follow some key data principles you'll have a lot more flexibility in what you can do with your data once it's entered.

Those principles are:

1. Use the first row of your worksheet to label your data.

2. List all of your data in continuous rows after that first row without including any subtotals or subheadings or anything that isn't your data. Keep all data for a specific item on one row. (So a customer buys something from you on July 1st, have all of the information related to that transaction on one single line if transactions are what you care about. Or have all information related to sales of Widgets on one line per transaction if what you care about is your widgets.)

3. To the extent possible, format your data in such a way that it can be analyzed. (Which means rather than put in a free-text field, try to use a standardized list of values instead. A column that uses a 1 to 5 point ranking scale is better for analysis than a column that uses a free text field where anyone can say anything.)

4. Standardize your values. Customer A should always be listed as Customer A. United States should always be United States not USA, U.S.A., or America.

5. Store your raw data in one location; analyze or correct it elsewhere.

I wrote an entire book on this subject, *How to Gather and Use Data for Business Analysis*, so if you really want to explore this topic, that's where you need to go. In the interim those were just my high-level rules to follow when possible.

Of course, some of the ways in which I use Excel don't conform to those principles. And that's fine.

My budgeting worksheet is more of a snapshot of information than a listing of data, so it doesn't follow most of these rules because it's a report. But my worksheet that lists all vendor payments for the year? You bet it's formatted using this approach.

I bring this up because it's important before you start collecting and entering data into Excel that you think about how you might use that data. Are you just wanting to display this information? Or do you want to analyze it?

When in doubt, assume that you'll want to analyze your information at some point and structure everything accordingly. Here is a good example of data that is formatted in a way that in can be easily analyzed:

	A	B	C	D
1	Customer Name	Amount Paid	Date	Customer Satisfaction Rating
2	Customer A	$ 250.00	January 1, 2020	3
3	Customer B	$ 125.00	February 3, 2022	4
4	Customer C	$ 132.00	June 1, 2021	5
5	Customer D	$ 287.00	July 8, 2020	3
6				
7				

It's not that you can't work with data that isn't set up using the rules above, it's just that it's harder to do.

Okay, now that we have that out of the way, what are some tricks you should know to make inputting or deleting data easier?

Enter Information In A Cell

To enter information or data into a cell in Excel, click into that cell and just start typing or paste in whatever it is you want to enter.

Edit Information In A Cell - F2

If there is already data in that cell and you want to edit it, I find using the F2 key helps. The F2 key will take you to the end of the contents of that cell. And then you can use the arrow keys to move within the contents of the cell and make whatever edits you need to make.

This is useful for when you don't want to completely overwrite what's already in there. For example, I sometimes will forget a closing paren when I enter a formula. Going to that cell, using F2, and then typing that closing paren is the quickest way to fix that issue.

However, not every computer is set up to have F2 be the default. I've had to change that on each new laptop I've bought over the last five years or so. If that's the case and your key that says F2 is actually controlling the volume on your computer, then you'll need to use the Fn key and the F2 key together.

Edit Information in A Cell – Other Options

Another option is to click on the cell and then click into the formula bar and edit the text that way. Once more, you can use the arrow keys to move through what's already there once you're clicked into that cell. Or you can click into the point in those cell contents where you want to make your edit.

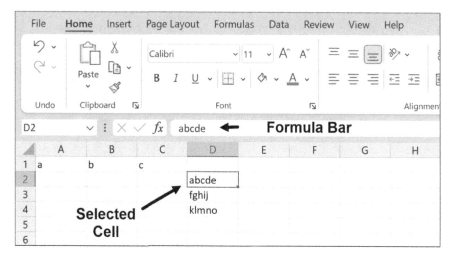

If you are working with formulas and cell references, when you click into the formula bar each cell reference will be color-coded and the corresponding cell in the worksheet will share that color.

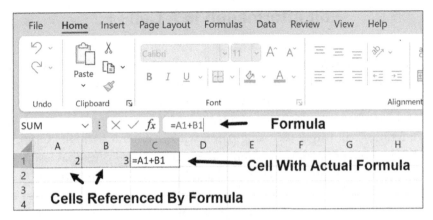

Undo

To undo something when you make a mistake, use Ctrl + Z. Learn this one.. Trust me.

I sometimes think I've done something the right way and as soon as I finish, I realize I was mistaken. Ctrl + Z quickly gets me back to where I was before I made that mistake.

And sometimes undoing what you did (like a bad sort that didn't include all columns) is the only way to safely fix things.

If you don't want to use that control shortcut, you can also click on the Undo option in the Undo section of the Home tab. It looks like an arrow pointing counter-clockwise.

That also gives you the option, if you click on the dropdown arrow instead, to undo multiple steps at once.

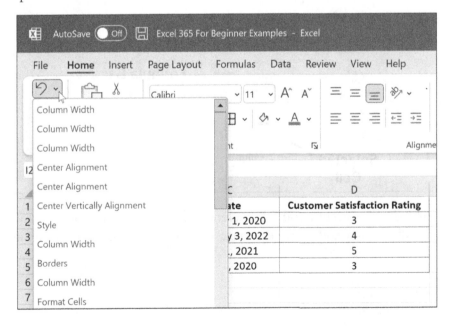

You can see the steps I took to create that data table in the image above. If I click on one of the items at the bottom of that list, Excel will undo every step from that point forward. So if I scroll down and find "Typing 'Customer Name' in A1" and click on that, it erases the table entirely and the worksheet goes back to how it was at that point in time.

Redo

Of course, you may find that you undo something that you didn't want to undo and have to bring it back. That's what Redo (Ctrl + Y) is for. That will bring back one step. But you can also go to the Undo section of the Home tab and click on the dropdown for Redo, which is an arrow rotating clockwise, and then choose from that list to bring back as many steps as you need to.

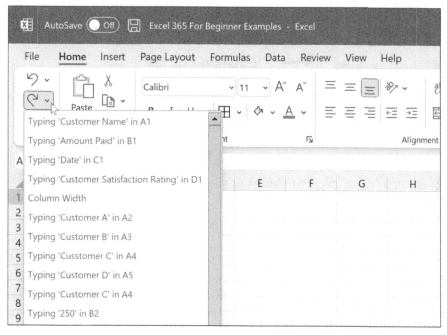

So I would scroll to the end of that list there and choose the very last option to restore my entire table.

Esc

Another handy tool to keep in mind is using the Esc key. Sometimes I will start entering information in a cell and then accidentally click somewhere I don't want to or in some other way get stuck doing something I don't want to be doing. If I'm mid-mistake, I use Esc to back up.

It basically says, "Oops, just kidding, let me stop doing this and go back, thanks." It comes in especially handy when working with formulas when an inadvertent click can change a formula in a way you did not want.

Use Auto-Suggested Text

If you're inputting a lot of data directly into Excel and that data is repetitive, auto-suggested text can save you a ton of time.

What it does is looks at the values you've already entered into a column and suggests how to complete an entry for you.

So if I'm selling Widgets, Whatchamacallits, and Whatsits and I have five hundred rows of data to enter, I don't have to type each full word each time.

I can start to type Widgets, W-I, and Excel will suggest that word for me if I've already used it. Like here:

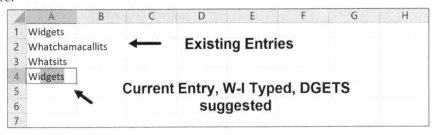

For that fourth entry, all I've typed so far are the W and the I, but Excel looked at the list of entries I already made and tried to complete the entry for me. I can ignore it and just keep typing or I can hit Enter to accept the suggestion. I only had to type two letters instead of seven, which is a great time-saver.

Now, there are some caveats here.

It tends to only look at entries that are connected. Meaning, if I had tried to type W-I in Row 5 but left Row 4 blank, Excel wouldn't make a suggestion. Unless I had a column next to this one that already had continuous entries in Rows 1 through 5. Basically, Excel needs some way to presume that the cell you're entering data into now is connected to the one above it before it will make a suggestion.

Also, what you type has to be unique for Excel to make a suggestion. So when I type W-I, Excel says "Widgets". But if I type "W-H" it's not going to do anything because that could be either Whatsits or Whatchamacallits. I'd have to type W-H-A-T-S or W-H-A-T-C before Excel suggested a word for me.

If you can, keep this in mind when creating your values. Because using Customer A, Customer B, Customer C doesn't save you any time. But using A Customer, B Customer, and C Customer would. (And if you find that funky, you could always later use data manipulation to turn "B Customer" into "Customer B" after you'd saved yourself a bunch of time inputting those entries.)

Excel also doesn't tend to be very good with pulling in rare values. Here, for example, I entered Whatchamacallit as my value for about 440 entries and then tried to type Widgets. I had to type W-I-D-G-E-T before Excel finally suggested Widgets as my value.

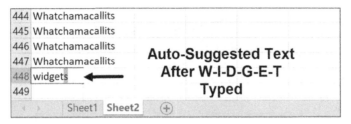

Excel also won't make suggestions for numeric values. So even if you have an entry like 123TRE, it won't even try to suggest a value until that first letter is typed. But once the first letter is typed it will look for a word to suggest.

Again, keep this in mind when coming up with values that you might input. You will save more time if you have TRE123 instead of 123TRE as the customer identifier as long as TRE is somewhat unique and you don't use TRE123, TRE456, TRE789. In which case you'd be better off sticking with 123TRE, 456TRE, and 789TRE.

Despite how confusing I probably just made that sound, it really is helpful when inputting values.

Copy Patterns or Repeated Entries

In the next chapter we'll discuss copying data in detail, but this is more of a tip related to inputting your data, so I wanted to cover it here.

Excel has the ability to recognize patterns. For example, let's say that you wanted to create a data table that shows your income for each month of a year. So you want Column A to have January, February, March, etc.

That is a pattern that Excel can recognize. Which means you do not have to enter all twelve months. You can actually type just January into the first cell, click back onto that cell, and then left-click and drag down from the bottom right corner. Your cursor should look like a little black plus sign as you do this and as you drag past each cell Excel is going to show you the value it predicts for that cell.

Here, for example, I have dragged down to Row 4 and Excel is telling me that will be April. As I dragged past Row 2 it showed February and for Row 3 it showed March.

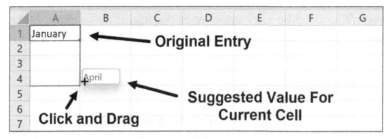

When I let up on that left-click and drag, Excel will then populate all of those fields for me. Like so:

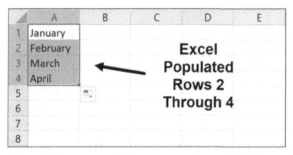

All I had to do was give Excel the start of the pattern. It took it from there.

Now that was click and drag. But if you already have other entries in your data table, then you don't even have to do that. You can double-left click on that bottom right corner and if Excel can see how far to take the entries down it will populate all those rows for you.

Here, for example, I have twelve rows that already have a year entered:

All I have to do is double left-click in the bottom right corner of the cell that says January in it and Excel does the rest for me.

Sometimes, though, you may just want to copy values down instead. For example, when I bring in my monthly sales reports from my various vendors I always add two columns, one for Month, and one for Year. In the first row of my data I put the Month and Year values. I then highlight both of those sells and double-left click in the corner.

Excel does its thing and populates the values for Month and Year for the rest of the entries in that table (which can be hundreds of entries). But it tries to turn them into a series. So January 2020 is followed by February 2021, etc.

That's not what I want. But it's an easy fix. I can click on the dropdown arrow for that Auto Fill Options that shows at the bottom right side of the series in the workspace and change the option from Fill Series to Copy Cells. That immediately changes all those values to January 2020 which is what I want. It's faster than copying the top entries, selecting all the other cells, then pasting, especially when there are a lot of entries. Although that works, too. (And is discussed in the next chapter.)

The examples I just showed you are for copying a pattern down a column, but it works just as well across a row. So you could write Monday in Cell A1 and then click and drag to the right from the bottom right corner of that cell to get the rest of the days of the week.

Excel can also recognize custom patterns, but you usually have to give it more than one entry for that. And it seems to be better with numbers than letters. So I can enter Customer 123, Customer 124, Customer 125, and then get it to predict Customer 126 and so on, but if I use Customer A, Customer B, Customer C, it can't see that pattern.

So sometimes it will help, sometimes it won't. But when it does help it's very helpful.

Display the Contents of a Cell As Text

Excel tries to be helpful, but sometimes it fails miserably. There's a reason there are numerous jokes on the internet about Excel mistaking things for dates. If you get anywhere close to entering information that it thinks might be a date, it will transform that entry into a numeric date and format it accordingly.

For example, I sometimes want to have "January 2020" in a cell in my worksheet as a label. As soon as I type that into that cell and hit Enter, Excel turns it into a date with a day of the week included.

My text entry of "January 2020" displays as Jan-20 in that cell and in the formula bar you can see it listed as 1/1/2020.

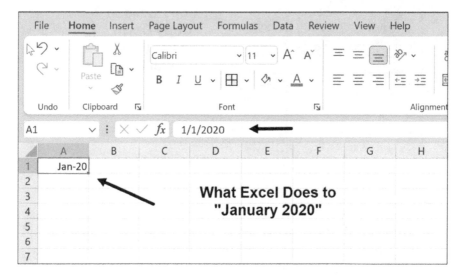

Not what I want.

The other time this happens is if you ever try to start an entry in a cell with a dash (-), a plus sign (+), or an equals sign (=), all of which Excel interprets as the beginning of a formula.

So if I want to use "- Item A" in a cell, I can't just type that in that cell. Excel will get very confused and give me a #NAME? error.

To keep Excel from reacting this way, you can type a single quote mark (') before the contents of the cell. If you do that, Excel will treat whatever you enter after that as text and will keep the formatting type as General. It also won't think that you're entering a formula in that cell that requires it to make a calculation.

For example, if you want to have June 2020 display in a cell in your worksheet, you need to type:

'June 2020

Not just

June 2020

If you want to have

- Item A

display in a cell, you need to type it as

'- Item A

The single quote mark will not be visible when you look at that cell in your worksheet or when you print the data from your worksheet. It is only visible in the formula bar when you've selected that cell. Like so:

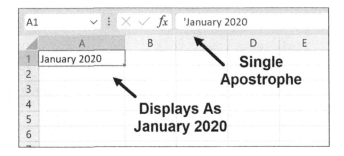

Include Line Breaks In a Cell

Another thing you might find yourself wanting to do is to include text in a cell but have it break across lines. So, for example, you may want an entry that looks like this:

	A	B	C	D	E
	A				
	B				
1	C				
2					
3					
4					
5					
6					

where the A, the B, and the C are all on separate lines. You can't just use Enter because that will take you to the next cell. What you have to do is use Alt + Enter. So hold down the Alt key as you hit Enter and that will create a line break within the cell.

Delete Data

To delete information you've entered into a single cell, simply click into that cell and use the Delete key. You can delete the text in more than one cell at a time the same way. Just select all of those cells and then use the Delete key.

This deletes the contents of the cell, but leaves the cell where it is.

You can also double-click on a cell or use F2 to get to the end of the contents in a cell and then use your computer's backspace key to delete the contents of a cell one character at a time.

Or you can click on a cell and then go to the formula bar and select a portion of the cell contents and then use Delete or Backspace.

Clear Cell Formatting

When you delete the the contents of a cell that does not remove the formatting that's been applied to that cell.

To delete the contents of a cell as well as the formatting, select the cell(s), go to the Editing section of the Home tab, click on the dropdown next to the Clear option, and choose to Clear All.

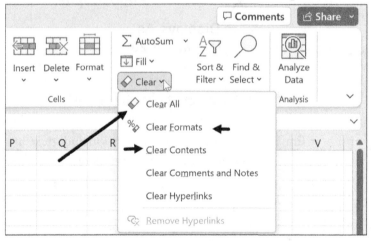

You can also choose to just Clear Formats or Clear Contents using that same dropdown menu.

Find and Replace

Find will locate whatever it is you're searching for. Replace takes that one step further and locates that entry and then replaces it with whatever you designate.

I don't use replace often in Excel, because I'm usually dealing with data entries and I don't want to risk messing those up. But I do use find fairly often to get to a particular entry in a data table.

(Another option, which we'll cover more later, is filtering. That one is best for displaying a subset of your data, especially when find would return more than one result.)

But back to find and replace. Let's walk through an example using replace.

Above I mentioned that typing in A Customer instead of Customer A would let Auto-Suggested text work in your favor. But having entries that say "A Customer" feels awkward. I could enter all of my entries using A Customer and then use Replace to change those over to Customer A. That's one way to fix that after the fact.

Here are some random entries to work with:

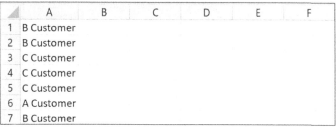

I actually have 51 rows of entries randomly assigned between A Customer, B Customer, and C Customer. I want to change those over to Customer A, Customer B, and Customer C.

Either Ctrl + F or Ctrl + H will open the Find and Replace dialogue box. Ctrl + F will open it to the Find tab, Ctrl + H will open it to the Replace tab.

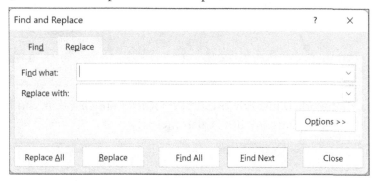

If you don't want to use the control shortcuts or you forget them, you can go to the Editing section of the Home tab and click on the dropdown arrow for Find & Select and then choose either Find or Replace from there.

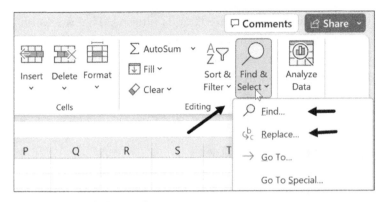

That will also open the same dialogue box.

The entries we're dealing with here are very basic. So we could probably just type A Customer in the Find What field and Customer A in the Replace With field and be fine clicking on Replace All.

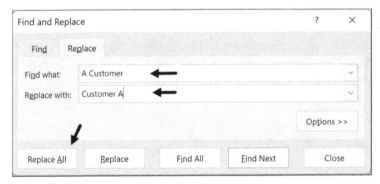

And, sure enough, that worked just fine on the 19 entries in my list that said A Customer. You can see two of those entries here are now Customer A.

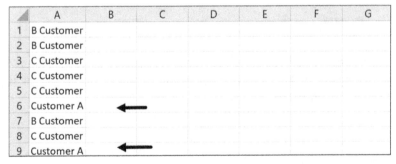

But you have to be careful with Replace. Because it is not, by default case sensitive. And it also does not, by default, look for whole words. So if I'd had entries that were AA Customer, for example, and I did a replace for A Customer, those entries would be changed, too. I would end up with entries that said ACustomer A, which is not what I want.

The way to make sure that Excel only replaces what you want it to replace is to click on that Options button to expand the Find and Replace dialogue box. Here is what that will look like:

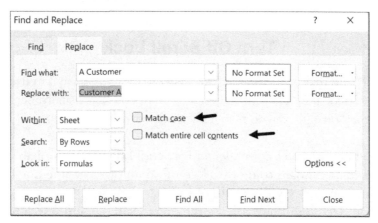

If I check the box for Match Entire Cell Contents, that addresses the issue with AA Customer versus A Customer. And if I check Match Case, that makes sure that if I have a paragraph of text in that worksheet that discusses "how a customer may want to…", I don't inadvertently replace that and end up with "how Customer A may want to…"

Replace in Excel is a fairly blunt tool as it currently exists. It is far more refined in Word where I do use it often. But wherever you use it, be sure you've really thought through what the replacement you're making will actually do to your contents.

When in doubt, you can use the Find option first to see which entries your current criteria capture. Here I clicked over to the Find tab, typed in my text, B Customer, under Find What, and then clicked on Find All. The Value column shows the contents of each cell in its entirety.

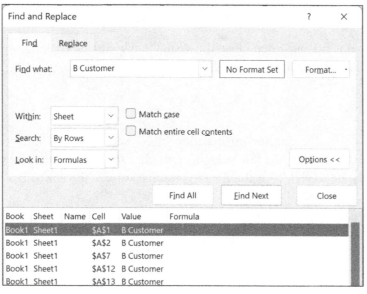

You can click on each entry in that list to go to it.

If you just want to walk through your results, you can use Find Next instead.

Turn Off Scroll Lock

On occasion I will find that navigating in Excel isn't working the way I'm used to. I arrow and things don't move like they should. When this happens, it's usually because Scroll Lock somehow was turned on. The way to turn it back off is to click on the Scroll Lock key on your keyboard.

Unfortunately, I haven't had a computer with a Scroll Lock key in probably a decade, so you have to open a virtual keyboard to do this. Use the Windows key (the one with four squares to the left of your spacebar) + Ctrl + O to open it.

(Another option is to go through your Start menu to Settings and search for keyboard there and then toggle the on-screen keyboard to on.)

The keyboard will appear on your screen. The Scroll Lock key (ScrLk) should be colored when it's turned on. It's one of the right-hand-side options on the keyboard:

 Click on it to turn it off and then close the virtual keyboard by clicking on the X in the top corner. Excel will return to acting normally.

* * *

Okay. That's the basics of entering information into Excel. I do still want to talk about how you enter formulas in Excel, but I'm going to save that for its own chapter where we discuss formulas at a very high-level. (For the detailed discussion you'll want to read *102 Useful Excel 365 Functions*.)

Now let's talk about copying, pasting, and moving data around.

Copy, Paste, and Move Data

Now that you know how to enter data into an Excel workbook it's time to talk about how you can move that data around.

Before we dive in on copy, cut, paste, etc. I want to refresh you on how to select cells. It was covered in the terminology section, but in case anyone skipped that…

Select Data

To select one cell, click on it or arrow to it.

To select multiple cells that are next to one another, go to a cell at the outer end of that range, hold down the Shift key, and then use the arrow keys to select your cells. Or left-click and drag with your mouse to select the remaining cells you want. You can select across rows, columns or both rows and columns.

To select multiple cells that are not next to one another, click on the first cell you want, and then hold down the Ctrl key as you click on the other cells you want. You cannot use the arrow keys for this one.

To select an entire column, click on the letter for that column.

To select an entire row, click on the number for that column.

To select multiple rows or columns it works the same as for cells. Shift and arrow or left-click and drag if they're next to each other, Ctrl if they aren't.

Select All

If you want to select all of the data in a worksheet, go to that worksheet and then use Ctrl + A.

If you don't want to use Ctrl + A, you can also click in the top left corner where the columns and rows meet.

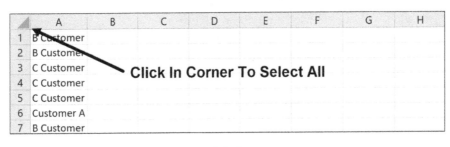

* * *

Now that you know how to select cells, rows, columns, or data, we can talk about copy, paste, and moving things around.

Copy and Move Data As Is To One Location

Let's start with copying data from one location to another without any special changes to that data.

When you Copy you leave an original version of the data where it was and you take that exact same data and you put a copy in a different location.

By default that data will transfer with all of its formatting. And if there were any formulas in the data you selected those formulas will move as well. (We'll come back to formulas more in the formulas section.)

So to copy and move data as is, first, select the data you want to copy.

Next, the easiest way to copy is to just use Ctrl + C. (If you only memorize a handful of Ctrl shortcuts, make this one of them.) That will take a copy of your data for you.

Go to where you want to put that data, click into the first cell in that range, and hit Enter.

Here, for example, I have copied the data from Cells A1 through A6 to Cells E1 through E6.

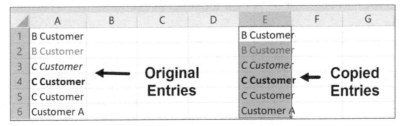

So I selected Cells A1 through A6, used Ctrl + C, went to Cell E1, and hit Enter. All of the text and all of the formatting copied over.

If you didn't want to use a Ctrl shortcut there are a number of other ways to access the copy option. One is to right-click on the selected cells and choose Copy from the dropdown menu.

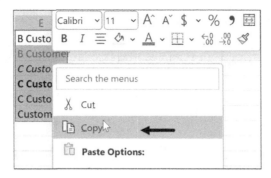

Another is to go to the Clipboard section of the Home tab and click on the Copy option from there.

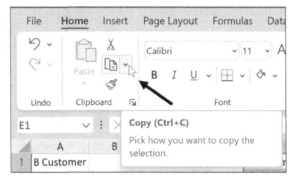

Copy and Move Data As Is To Multiple Locations

If you want to copy and move the same data but to multiple locations, then you'll want to use the Paste function instead of Enter to place the data in each new location.

So copy it the same as before, but when you click into the first cell of the new range use Ctrl + V instead to paste the data. (This is another Ctrl shortcut you should absolutely memorize.)

Look at these copied and pasted entries. It may be a little hard to see, but the copied entries have a dotted line around them:

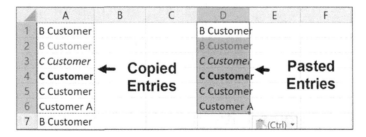

This means that they are still copied even though I pasted them once into Column D, so I can go to another location and paste them again. As long as I use Ctrl + V (or one of the other ways to paste that I'll discuss in just a moment) I can put that copied data into as many locations as I want.

When you are done copying your data, use the Esc key to turn that off. Typing into a new cell will work as well.

Just like with Copy, Paste can also be found by right-clicking on the selected cell(s) or going to the Clipboard section of the Home tab.

Move Data To A New Location

If you don't want to take a copy of your data, but instead want to move that data to somewhere new so that there's just that one copy of the data in the new location only, then you need to use Cut. It works the same as Copy, you select your data, Cut, and then go to the new location, and put the data there.

The control shortcut for this is Ctrl + X. (Another good one to memorize.) And it works with either Enter or Ctrl + V at the new location.

But with Cut you are moving that data and you can only move it once. So both Paste and Enter place the data and you're done.

Here is data I Cut from Cells A1 through A6 and Pasted into Cells C1 through C6:

	A	B	C	D	E	F	G
1			B Customer				
2			B Customer				
3	**Old**		C Customer	←	**New**		
4	**Location**		C Customer		**Location**		
5			C Customer				
6			Customer A				
7	B Customer						

I went to Cells A1 through A6 and selected them, used Ctrl + X, clicked into Cell C1, and used Ctrl + V. Note that there is now no content in Cells A1 through A6. It is only in Cells C1 through C6.

Cutting also takes the cell formatting with it. So if I type a new value in Cell A2 which previously had red text in it, that text is black not red.

You can Cut by selecting the cells and then right-clicking and choosing Cut from the dropdown menu or by going to the Clipboard section of the Home tab. Cut is shown as a pair of scissors in the Clipboard section.

Copying or Cutting Cells With Formulas

If you have formulas in the data you're moving you need to be more careful because the choice to Cut versus the choice to Copy will impact your result, but I'm going to save that for the

Formulas chapter. Just note for now that there is an issue there that you need to be aware of.

Copy and Move Data With Changes

Sometimes you will want to copy just the contents of a cell without keeping any of its formatting. Or you will want to take a list of values in a column and put them into a single row instead. Or maybe you want the results of a formula, but you don't want to keep the formula anymore.

That's where the Paste Special options come in handy.

First, know that you can only use Paste Special if you've copied the contents of a cell (Ctrl + C). These options do not work if you've cut the contents of a cell (Ctrl + X).

To Paste Special, you either need to right-click in the new cell and choose from the Paste Options section in that dropdown menu

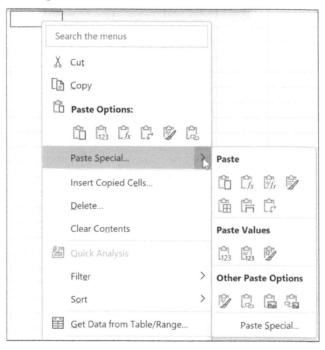

Or you need to click on the dropdown arrow under Paste in the Clipboard section of the Home tab.

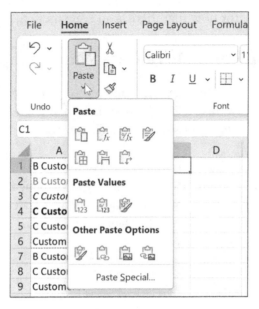

Clicking on Paste Special at the bottom of either of those lists will open the Paste Special dialogue box, but you're rarely going to need that.

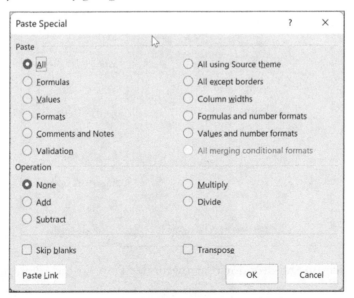

If you use the dropdown menu you can actually see what the result will be by holding your mouse over each option. Here, for example, I have my cursor over Paste Values and you can see that it will paste in the text that I've copied from Column A but without any of the formatting such as bolding, italics, or red text color.

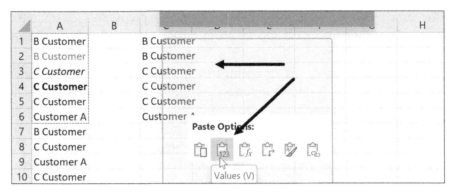

And here is what Paste Transpose looks like in preview:

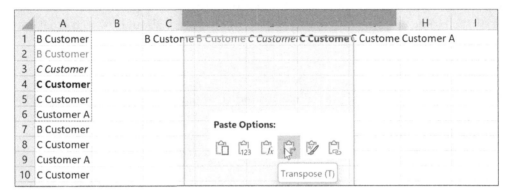

Those are the two paste options I use the most.

Paste Values has a 123 in the bottom corner of the clipboard image and what it lets you do is copy entries and then just paste those values. This is incredibly useful when working with formulas. For example, I would've probably fixed that transform B Customer to Customer B problem using one of two functions, TEXTJOIN or CONCATENATE. But that means I would've been doing so using a formula. And that formula would have depended on the content of cells in two different columns that I would have wanted to delete.

The only way to delete those columns but keep my "calculation" result would be to copy that column with my final calculation and then paste-values so that I keep the result of the "calculation" but not the formula.

It's also useful when you want the contents of a cell, but would prefer to use the formatting in the destination cell(s). For example, if you're copying from one Excel file to another.

Another way I use it is when I've run a set of calculations on my data, found my values, and now want to sort or do something else with my data but don't want to risk having the values change on me.

I will highlight the entire data set, copy, and then paste special-values right over the top of my existing data. (Just be sure to type Esc after you do this so that the change is fixed in place.)

I often do that when dealing with pivot tables. I'll create a pivot table to summarize my data, but then I copy that table and paste-special so that it's no longer a pivot table but just the calculated values.

The Paste Transpose option—the one with two sets of arrows in the bottom corner—is very useful if you have a row of data that you want to turn into a column of data or a column of data that you want to turn into a row.

Like in the screenshot above where you can see that my six entries that were in a column would be in a single row across six columns if I chose that option.

Just be sure before you paste that there isn't any data that will be overwritten when you paste your entries, because Excel won't warn you before it overwrites it.

There are a lot more paste options available, but those are the two main ones I use. I do also use paste formatting, but I do that through the Format Painter option in the Clipboard section of the Home tab. We'll discuss that more when we talk about how to format your data.

* * *

Now let's talk about another way to move around your data which is by inserting cells, rows, and columns. Also, I want to talk about worksheets a bit more, namely renaming them to reflect what they contain and also moving or copying them.

I'm going to start with worksheets, because that's the easiest part.

Rename a Worksheet

To rename an Excel worksheet, double-click on the worksheet name, and then start typing the new name you want to use. If you change your mind, use the Esc key to back out.

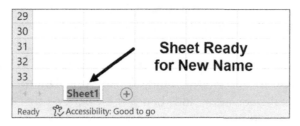

You can also right-click on the tab with the name and choose Rename from the dropdown menu.

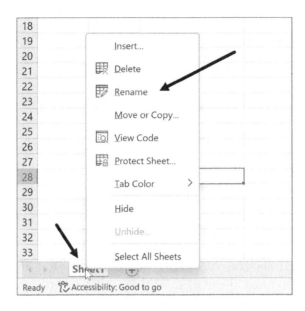

There are rules to naming worksheets. It can't be blank. It also has to be 31 character or less. And those characters cannot include / \ ? * : [or] and the worksheet name cannot begin or end with an apostrophe ('). Also, no worksheet can be named History because behind the scenes Excel already has one of those in each worksheet.

Don't worry too much about those rules. In more recent versions of Excel they just won't let you type those prohibited characters. And if you accidentally leave the name blank it will show a dialogue box telling you there's an error with the name. You just need to click OK on that and type in an actual name. Use Esc to go back to the original name.

Add a Worksheet

To add a new worksheet you can click on the little plus sign next to the last existing worksheet. That will add a worksheet to the right of the last worksheet you were clicked on.

Or you can go to the Cells section of the Home tab, click on the dropdown arrow under Insert, and choose Insert Sheet. That will insert a worksheet to the left of the one you were clicked on before you chose that option.

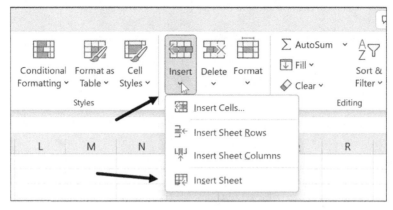

Move a Worksheet

To move a worksheet, left-click on the tab for the worksheet name and drag the worksheet to where you want it. As you move the worksheet there will be a little arrow pointing at the spot between the two worksheets where it would move to.

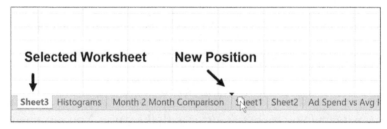

You can also right-click on the worksheet name and choose the Move or Copy option. That will bring up the Move or Copy dialogue box.

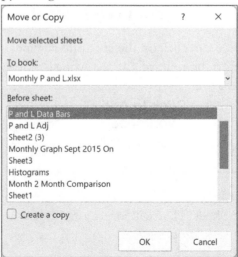

Click on the name of the worksheet you want to place the worksheet *before* and then click on OK. If you want to move a worksheet to another workbook you can do that from the Move or Copy dialogue box as well. Just change the option under To Book using that dropdown. Your available options will be a new Excel workbook or any Excel workbooks that are currently open.

Copy a Worksheet

You can also use the Move or Copy dialogue box to make a copy of a worksheet. I often will do this to put a copy of a worksheet I create in one workbook in a new workbook. To do so, click on the Create a Copy checkbox.

Here I've done so and selected to copy it to a new workbook using the dropdown menu choices. I just need to click OK to make that happen.

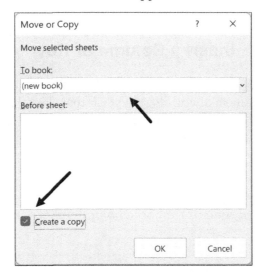

If you are moving or copying a worksheet to a new workbook and it includes formulas that reference other worksheets in the old workbook it will continue to reference to the old workbook. So be very careful about that, because if someone doesn't have access to the old workbook, those formulas aren't going to work for them.

(In general, I think it's best to keep everything contained in one workbook when working with formulas, but I know there are situations where that isn't possible. All I can say is, if you're going to have formulas that work across workbooks do so deliberately not just because it was a sloppy error.)

Delete a Worksheet

You can also delete a worksheet. To do so, right-click on the worksheet name and choose Delete from the dropdown menu.

Or you can go to the Cells section of the Home tab, click on the dropdown arrow for Delete, and choose Delete Sheet from there.

If the worksheet was blank, Excel will just delete it. If it contains any data Excel will show you a pop-up window asking you to confirm that you want to delete that worksheet. Be sure you really want to delete that worksheet, because you won't be able to undo it if you change your mind later.

* * *

That was worksheets, now let's talk about inserting and deleting columns, rows, and cells.

Insert a Column or Row

You only need to insert a column or row if you already have data in your worksheet and realize that you want a new column or row in the midst of that data that already exists. (Because, remember, the number of columns and rows in a worksheet is constant. So when you "insert" a column or row what you're really doing is just shifting around your existing data on that column and row map. You're taking data in Column A and moving it to Column B, but the total of columns in the worksheet isn't going to change.)

You have a number of options for this one.

I usually right-click on the letter for the column or number for the row and choose Insert from the dropdown menu.

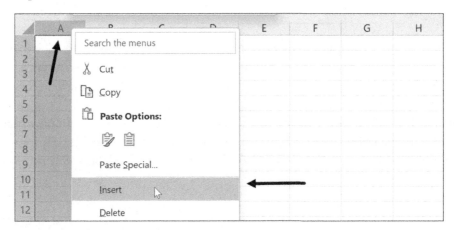

This will, for columns, insert a new column where I right-clicked and shift all of the data that was in that column previously or that was in any column to the right of that column over by one column. So if I right-click on Column B, all data that was in Column B is now in Column C, all data from Column C moves to Column D, etc.

You can insert multiple columns using this approach. Left-click on the column where you want to insert those new columns and then drag until you've selected the desired number of new columns to insert. Right-click and choose Insert from the dropdown. That should insert X number of columns and shift everything to the right.

Here you can see this for rows.

	A	B	C	D	E	F	G	H
1	1	2	3	4	5			
2								
3			←					
4								
5								
6								
7	6	7	8	9	10			
8	11	12	13	14	15			
9								

I selected Rows 2 through 6, then right-clicked and chose Insert. That moved the values from Rows 2 and 3 (the numbers 6 through 10 and 11 through 15) down that many rows so that they are now in Rows 7 and 8. Rows are always added above the selection, so everything shifts down.

You can also insert a column or row by right-clicking in a single cell that's in that row or column and choosing Insert from the dropdown menu. Excel won't know whether you want to insert a cell, row, or column, so it will show you the Insert dialogue box.

Click Entire Row or Entire Column and then choose OK to insert a row or column, respectively.

Your final option is to select a row or column or click into a cell in that row or column and then go to the Cells section of the Home tab and choose Insert Sheet Rows or Insert Sheet Columns from the dropdown menu.

Insert a Cell

Inserting a cell works much the same way. Click where you want to insert that cell, right-click, and choose Insert. Or click where you want to insert that cell and go to the Cells section of the Home tab, click on the Insert dropdown arrow, and choose Insert Cells.

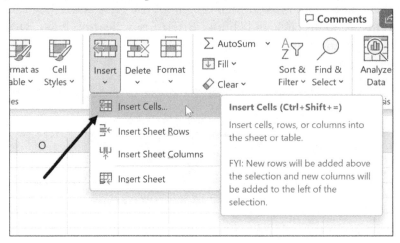

There is one quirk with inserting cells, however, and that's that you have to tell Excel whether to shift things to the right or to shift things down to make room. So you will always see the Insert dialogue box.

If you choose to Shift Cells Right, all data in that row with that cell will move to the right one column. If you choose to Shift Cells Down, all data in that column with that cell will move down one row.

Which you want will depend on the data you already have in your worksheet and why you're adding this cell.

You can insert multiple cells at once, which is what I often do. Just select the cell range first (left-click and drag) and then choose to insert.

Be careful when adding cells into a worksheet as opposed to entire rows or columns. I have, more than once, added say five cells and shifted my data but forgotten that I had other data in that same column or row in my worksheet and accidentally moved my data out of alignment.

So when adding cells, check first to see what is impacted. And check again after to make sure everything looks okay. If you get it wrong, Ctrl + Z, for Undo, is your friend. It will undo what you just did and let you try again. (Ctrl + Y is Redo if you ever undo something and decide that wasn't necessary.)

Delete Rows, Columns, or Cells

Deleting works just like inserting. Select the row, column, or cells that you want to delete and then either right-click and choose Delete from the dropdown or go to the Cells section of the Home tab, click on the dropdown for Delete, and choose your option there.

As with inserting cells, when you delete cells you should see a dialogue box that looks just like the insert one except it's talking about deleting. You will again need to decide whether to shift cells, this time left and up are the two choices.

So look at your other data and decide what to do. You may need to delete a range of cells instead of one single cell to keep everything in alignment.

If you select a range of cells and try to use the Delete key that will just delete your data, but the cells will remain there so none of the rest of your data will move.

Also, be careful with deleting rows, columns, or cells that have data in them. Check any formulas in your worksheet to see if deleting that data impacted those formulas. It will usually show up as a #REF! error.

Here, for example, I had a value in Cell A1 and a value in Cell B1 that were then added together in Cell C1. When I deleted Column A, that removed that value that was being used in the formula so the formula no longer works.

B1		⌄ ⋮ ✕ ✓	fx	=#REF!+A1			
	A	B	C	D	E	F	G
1	3	#REF!					
2							
3							
4							
5							
6							
7							

Note also that the value that was in Cell B1 moved to Cell A1 and that my formula that was in Cell C1 moved to Cell B1. Everything shifted one column. (One of the nice things about Excel is that the formula automatically updated to reflect that shift. So the formula now shows A1 not B1 for that second value location.)

Formulas and Functions

We've touched on formulas and functions a couple of times now, but I've set that aside each time. If you really want to dig in on formulas and functions in Excel I wrote a whole book about it that includes over a hundred different Excel functions and how each one works, *102 Useful Excel 365 Functions*.

But formulas are such a key part of working in Excel that I also want to talk about them here. So some of what I'm going to cover here duplicates the introductory material in that book. But it's a higher-level discussion than you get there. And we certainly are not going to cover a hundred functions here.

Cell Notation

Before we can move forward with a discussion of formulas, we need to talk in more depth about cell notation because cell notation is how you tell Excel where your data is for your formula.

I already discussed in the terminology section how each cell is identified by the combination of its Column and Row and that you should think of that as map coordinates. So Cell A1 is the first column, first row of a worksheet.

Within Excel when you are referencing that cell, you leave off the Cell portion. So you just write A1.

You can also reference multiple cells at once. To reference a cell range, so all the cells between X point and Y point, you use a colon to separate the first coordinate from the last. If I write

A1:A25

that's all cells between Cell A1 and Cell A25. If I write

A1:B25

that's all cells in Columns A and B and from Rows 1 through 25.

If you want to reference cells that aren't touching or that don't form a clean rectangular shape, then you need to use commas to separate the cells or ranges.

A1,B2,C3

would be referencing Cells A1, B2, and C3. And

A1:A3,B1:B6

would be referencing the combination of Cells A1 through A3 and Cells B1 through B6.

Excel also has ways of identifying which worksheet those cells are in if you're referring to cells in a different worksheet. This is done by writing the name of the worksheet followed by an exclamation point before the cell reference.

Sheet2!C19

is referring to Cell C19 in the worksheet called Sheet2.

You can also identify which workbook a cell is in using brackets.

[Book1]Sheet3!E11

is referring to Cell E11 in the worksheet called Sheet3 in the workbook called Book1.

I have never bothered to memorize how to reference worksheets or workbooks, because Excel will write that for you if you start a formula and then go to that workbook or worksheet and select the cells you want to use. So I always let Excel do that heavy lifting for me.

You can also reference an entire column using the : like so:

A:A

is referencing Column A and

A:C

is referencing Columns A, B, and C.

Same goes for Rows.

1:1

is referencing all cells in Row 1

1:5

is referencing all cells in Rows 1 through 5.

Okay, now that you have an understanding of how to tell Excel where your data is located, let's define formulas and functions.

Definition of Formulas and Functions

For our purposes I'm going to define a formula in Excel as anything that is started with an equals sign and asks Excel to perform a calculation or task.

(Technically, you can start a formula with a plus or a minus sign as well, but I'm just going to ignore that because unless you're coming from a specific background where you learned to do things that way, you shouldn't do that. Also, Excel transforms those formulas into ones that use an equals sign anyway.)

I define a function as a command that is used within a formula to give instructions to Excel to perform a pre-defined task or set of tasks.

Think of a function in Excel as agreed-upon shorthand for some task.

Examples of Formulas and Functions

A formula in Excel could be as basic as:

$$=A1$$

It starts with an equals sign and is telling Excel that this particular cell where we've written our formula should have the exact same value as Cell A1. The "task" Excel completes here is pulling in that value.

But usually a formula will be more complex than that. For example:

$$=SUM(A1,B1,C1)$$

which could also be written as

$$=SUM(A1:C1)$$

is telling Excel to take the values in the specified cells and sum them together. So if the value in Cell A1 is 2, and the value in Cell B1 is 3, and the value in Cell C1 is 4, then this formula would return a value of 9.

You can also combine multiple functions or calculations within a single formula. Each cell can only hold one formula, but that formula can perform multiple tasks. For example,

$$=ROUND(RAND()*100,0)$$

is a formula that combines three steps to randomly generate a number between 0 and 100. It includes two functions, RAND and ROUND, as well as one mathematical calculation.

RAND generates a random number between 0 and 1. The *100 part takes that result and turns it into a value between 0 and 100. ROUND takes that result and rounds that number to a whole number.

How to Create a Formula

The basic rules of building a formula are to (a) start with an equals sign, (b) always use an opening paren after a function name, and (c) if you use an opening paren make sure that it's paired with a closing paren.

Functions always require opening and closing parens, but you can also have opening and closing parens when doing pure math, too. So

$$=234*(123+345+(2*3))$$

is a perfectly valid Excel formula that is telling Excel to multiply 2 times 3 and then add that to 123 and 345 and then take that total and multiply it times 234. It's straight out of math class.

Functions normally require additional inputs, but not always. In our example above with ROUND and RAND, RAND is a function that does not use other inputs. It just has an opening paren followed by a closing paren.

But ROUND does have inputs. And everything between that opening paren after ROUND and the closing paren at the end of that formula are those inputs. In the case of RAND the first input is the number to be rounded. In this case, that was the randomly generated number times 100. The second input is how many places to round that number to. Since I wanted a whole number that was 0.

For each function you use, Excel will help you with which inputs are required. If I type

$$=ROUND($$

into Excel, the minute I type that opening paren it tells me what the inputs are that are required for that function. Like so:

If that isn't enough information for me, because maybe I'm not familiar with the function, I

can click on the function name in that little display box and it will open a dialogue box or Help text on the function that gives more information.

Formulas do not have to start with a function or a calculation.

$$=A1+SUM(B1:B5)$$

is a perfectly legitimate formula that takes the value in Cell A1 and adds that to the values in Cells B1 through B5.

Your Result

After you enter your formula in your cell, hit enter or leave the cell by arrowing, using the tab key, or clicking away. That will be when Excel tries to calculate your result.

The cell where you entered your formula will then display the result of the formula.

The formula can still be seen and edited via the formula bar. So if you click back on that cell you will see the value in the cell, but the formula in the formula bar. Like so:

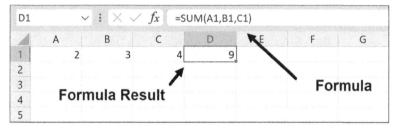

Here you can see that the result of adding Cells A1, B1, and C1 was 9 and that the formula used for that was

$$=SUM(A1,B1,C1)$$

You can also double-click into the cell with the formula or into the formula bar and Excel will color code each cell reference within the formula and within the worksheet so that you can make sure that the right cells were referenced in the formula.

It's a little hard to see in print, but Cells A1, B1, and C1 are each shaded a different color which corresponds to the color they are in the formula bar. This makes it easy to see which cell is being used in which part of a formula. That becomes especially helpful when dealing with very complex formulas.

Be careful moving away from a cell that has a formula in it. The best bet is to exit the cell using Esc. Otherwise sometimes Excel will try to select a new range of cells to use in the formula instead of just leaving the cell. This is especially an issue when using the arrow keys.

When you exit a cell that contains a formula, the cell will return to showing the calculated value not the formula.

Basic Math Calculations

Now let's talk about how to perform some basic math calculations in Excel.

Addition

If you want to add two numerical values together in Excel, you can use the plus sign (+) to indicate addition.

Here I'm adding 2 to 3:

$$=2+3$$

If those values were already showing in other cells, let's say Cells A1 and B1, you could write the formula to reference those cells instead:

$$=A1+B1$$

If you use cell notation, like in the second example there, then any change you make to the values in Cells A1 and B1 will also change the result of your formula because your formula is no longer performing a fixed calculation, like 2+3, but is instead performing a conditional calculation based on what's in Cells A1 and B1.

If you have more than two numbers to add together you can keep using the plus sign, so:

$$=A1+B1+C1$$

would add the values in Cells A1, B1, and C1. But it's better at that point to use the SUM function which will add all values included in the function. So:

$$=SUM(A1:C1)$$

adds the values in Cells A1, B1, and C1 together.

$$=SUM(A:A)$$

adds all the values in Column A.

$$=SUM(1:1)$$

adds all the values in Row 1.

If you ever forget how to write a cell range or to refer to an entire column or row, just start your formula, like this:

$$=SUM($$

and then go select the cells you want. Excel will write the reference for you and then you just need to close out the function with the closing paren.

Subtraction

To subtract one number from another you use the minus (-) sign. There is no function that will make this one easier, because the order of the values matters. Two minus three is not the same as three minus two.

However, you can combine the minus sign with the SUM function. So:

$$=A1-SUM(B1:D1)$$

is the equivalent of

$$=A1-B1-C1-D1$$

Multiplication

To multiply numbers you can use the asterisk (*) sign. Or you can use the function PRODUCT. All of the following will get the same result:

$$=A1*B1$$

$$=PRODUCT(A1:B1)$$

$$=PRODUCT(A1,B1)$$

Division

To divide two numbers you use the forward slash (/). There is no corresponding function because, again, order matters. Two divided by three is not the same as three divided by two. So:

$$=A1/B1$$

is the value in Cell A1 divided by the value in Cell B1.

* * *

To summarize:

Calculation	Numeric Symbol	Function	Examples
Addition	+	SUM	=A1+A2 =SUM(A1:A2)
Subtraction	-		=A1-A2
Multiplication	*	PRODUCT	=A1*A2 =PRODUCT(A1,A2)
Division	/		=A1/A2

A Quick Tip

Often when I just need to see the sum of values in a range of cells, I won't even write a formula or function. I'll just select those cells and look in the bottom right corner of my workspace. By default Excel displays the average, count, and sum of a range of selected cells in the very bottom right corner of the workspace.

(You can right-click where the values are displayed and also choose to have it display minimum and maximum values.)

Where To Find Functions

To find the functions available in Excel, you can go to the Formulas tab. There is a section called Function Library that lists various categories of functions. Mine shows Recently Used, Financial, Logical, Text, Date & Time, Lookup & Reference, Math & Trig, and then there's a dropdown for More Functions that shows the categories Statistical, Engineering, Cube, Information, Compatibility, and Web.

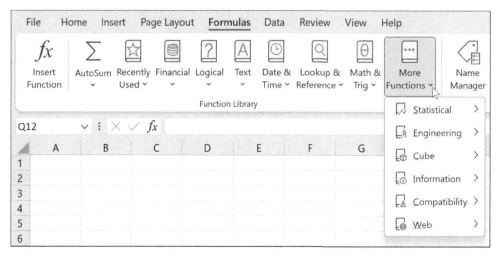

Click on the dropdown arrow under any of the categories and you'll see a listing of functions that fall under that heading. But, unless you know what you're looking for, that listing probably won't help you much because the functions are named things like ACCRINT and IFNA.

You *can* hold your cursor over each of the names and Excel *will* provide a brief description of the function for you, but for some of the lists that's a lot of functions to look through.

Each description also includes a Tell Me More at the end of the description. If you click on that option, the Excel Help task pane should appear. You can then click on the category for that function and choose the function from the list you see there to see further discussion of the function and examples of how to use it.

The level of detail provided varies by function. Sometimes it is very useful to read the Help section for a function and sometimes…it is not.

The approach I normally take instead is to click into the cell where I want to add my formula and then use the Insert Function option available on the far left-hand side of the Formulas tab.

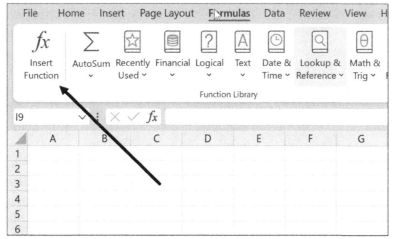

That brings up the Insert Function dialogue box.

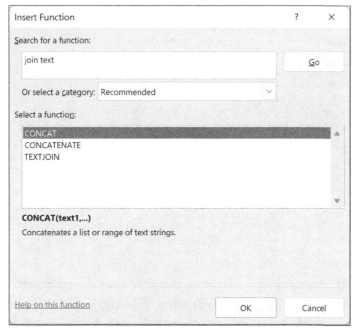

In the top section where it says "Search for a function" you can type what you're looking to do and then click on Go like I have above with "join text". (Be sure that the category dropdown right below the search box is set to All unless you know for sure what category your function falls under. After you click on Go that will turn into Recommended like it did in the image above.)

Excel will provide a list of functions that it thinks meet your search criteria. Sometimes this list is very far off, so don't just accept the first choice blindly.

You can left-click on each of the listed functions to see a brief description of the function directly below the box where the functions are listed. In the image above, that's showing for the CONCAT function.

You will also see in the description for each function a list of the required inputs for that function. For CONCAT that's at least one text entry.

If you need more information on a function, you can click on the "Help on this function" link in the bottom left corner of the dialogue box which will bring up help specific to that function.

Otherwise, you can just click on the function you want and choose OK, which will insert the function into whichever cell you were clicked into before you chose Insert Function. Excel will also open a Function Arguments dialogue box that lists the inputs your function needs and provides a location for you to input those values so that Excel can build your formula for you.

Here is the Function Arguments dialogue box for the TEXTJOIN function:

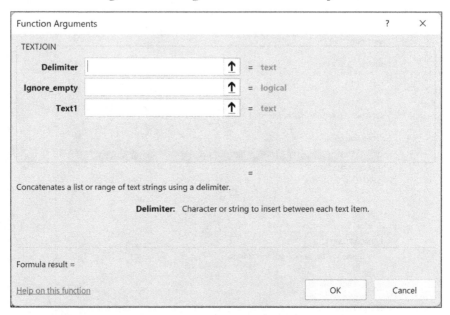

If you use the dialogue box, click into each input field and either input numeric values, cell references, or select the cells you want to use for each field. As you do so, Excel will show you a sample result based upon the inputs you've chosen at the bottom of the dialogue box next to Formula Result.

If you use the dialogue box, when you're done, click OK and the calculated value will appear in your cell.

If you don't want to use the dialogue box, close it out by clicking on OK and then OK on the error message that will appear.

This will give you the function in your cell in a formula format but without any of the required inputs, like so:

=TEXTJOIN()

Your cursor will be in the empty space between the opening and closing parens and you can then manually add the inputs at that point. Excel will show you which inputs are required and in which order.

If you X out the dialogue box instead, you'll just have a blank cell with no function or formula started.

* * *

That's about all I want to cover on how to write formulas and functions in this book. You can do a lot with basic addition, subtraction, multiplication, and division in Excel. And you now have an idea of where to look if you want to get fancier than that. And, of course, the third book in this series, *102 Useful Excel 365 Functions*, is almost two hundred pages long and covers over a hundred of the most useful functions in Excel.

But the other thing we need to cover when it comes to formulas is what makes them really powerful, and that's how you can copy formulas so that they apply to multiple cells.

Let's do that now.

Copying Formulas

The way in which formulas copy in Excel is key to what makes them so powerful. That's because you can write a formula once, copy it, and paste it to thousands of cells, and Excel will automatically adjust that formula to each new location

It's fantastic.

Let's say, for example, that I want to calculate total cost based upon units sold and price per unit for a thousand rows of data. Here are what the first few rows look like:

	A	B	C
1	**Units**	**Cost Per Unit**	**Total Cost**
2	2	$1.65	
3	4	$1.32	
4	3	$6.95	
5	6	$7.80	
6	9	$4.90	

I have units in Column A, cost per unit in Column B, and I want a total cost for each row in Column C.

The formula for Cell C2 in that first row is:

$$=A2*B2$$

Now, here's where the beauty of Excel comes in. I click on Cell C2 where I wrote that formula and then I double-left click in the bottom right corner of that cell and Excel copies my formula down for me.

(I could also use Ctrl + C, select the cell range and then use Ctrl + V or Enter to copy and paste my formula.)

Here's what I now have:

	A	B	C
1	Units	Cost Per Unit	Total Cost
2	2	$1.65	$3.29
3	4	$1.32	$5.28
4	3	$6.95	$20.84
5	6	$7.80	$46.81
6	9	$4.90	$44.11
7	3	$0.82	$2.47

Let's go to the Formula Auditing section of the Formulas tab and click on Show Formulas so we can see what Excel did for us.

	A	B	C
1	Units	Cost Per Unit	Total Cost
2	2	1.6452643749914	=A2*B2
3	4	1.3203471105506	=A3*B3
4	3	6.9475273087147	=A4*B4
5	6	7.80121230326684	=A5*B5
6	9	4.90149762880339	=A6*B6
7	3	0.824543582413774	=A7*B7

As Excel copied that first formula from Cell C2 down to Cells C3, C4, etc. it changed the formula. When the formula was copied one cell down from the original the cell references were updated to also reference cells one down.

So the original formula in Cell C2 used

$$=A2*B2$$

but when that was copied down to Cell C3 Excel changed that to

$$=A3*B3$$

Each cell reference in the formula adjusted relative to the original position.

Which is great for our thousand rows of data. It means we can write that formula once and copy it down and it works for all thousand rows of data.

Perfect.

But there are going to be times when you don't want Excel to adjust your formula for you. When that happens you need to either use fixed cell references or cut the formula and move it instead of copy and paste it. Let's start with fixed cell references.

Fixed Cell References

Let's take this scenario we've been working with and add a fixed 5% tax that needs to apply to every transaction. Here's our new data table:

	A	B	C	D	E	F	G	H
1	Units	Cost Per Unit	Total Cost	With Taxes		Tax Rate	5%	
2	2	$1.65	$3.29	$3.46				
3	4	$1.32	$5.28					
4	3	$6.95	$20.84					
5	6	$7.80	$46.81					
6	9	$4.90	$44.11					

Column D is calculating for that first transaction the total cost when we include a 5% tax. The formula is:

$$=C2*(1+G1)$$

where C2 is the cost before tax and G1 is the tax rate. If I copy that down to the other cells right now, Excel will adjust the cell references for both C2 and G1. I want it to do so for C2, but not for G1. I want every formula in my worksheet to continue to reference that tax rate in Cell G1.

To tell Excel to keep a cell reference fixed, I need to use dollar signs ($). That tells Excel, don't change this one. Keep it as is. And since I want to refer to that one specific cell, then the way to write that is:

$$=C2*(1+\$G\$1)$$

That means don't change the column or the row from G1 when you copy this.

Once I make that change to my formula, I can copy that formula down to all my other rows and have no issue.

	A	B	C	D	E	F	G
1	**Units**	**Cost Per Unit**	**Total Cost**	**With Taxes**		**Tax Rate**	0.05
2	2	1.6452643749914	=A2*B2	=C2*(1+$G$1)			
3	4	1.3203471105506	=A3*B3	=C3*(1+$G$1)			
4	3	6.9475273087147	=A4*B4	=C4*(1+$G$1)			
5	6	7.80121230326684	=A5*B5	=C5*(1+$G$1)			

Here you can see that I've double-clicked on Cell D4 to confirm that the formula is still referencing my tax rate in Cell G1. Perfect.

You can fix either the column reference for a cell, the row reference for a cell, or both. Just use the $ sign in front of whichever part of the cell reference you want to fix.

Moving a Formula

What happens if you're perfectly happy with a formula as written, but you just don't want it to display in the cell it's currently in? Sometimes, for example, I'll write a formula below a table of data and then later decide that I'd rather have all calculations off to the side of the table instead of below it.

I can't just copy that formula, because when I copy the formula and move it, all the cell references will change.

The way to get around this is to Cut the formula instead. So click on the original location, Ctrl + X, go to the new location, Ctrl + V. Esc. Or Ctrl + X, go to the new location, Enter.

If you just want the text of the formula as it exists right now but you don't want to move the original calculation, click on the cell, go to the formula bar, use Ctrl + A to select all of the text, use Ctrl + C to copy the selected text, Esc to exit that cell, click on the new location, and then use Ctrl + V to paste the text. (This is, for example, how I've copied the formulas into this book from the sample Excel worksheets where I wrote the formulas.)

* * *

Okay. Now that we've covered inputting your data and formulas, let's talk about how to make your data presentable. Because raw data in Excel is not pretty.

Formatting

If you're going to spend any amount of time working in Excel then you need to learn how to format cells, because inevitably your column won't be as wide as you want it to be or you'll want to have a cell with red-colored text or to use bolding or italics or something that isn't Excel's default.

That's what this section is for. It's an alphabetical listing of different things you might want to do to format your data in Excel.

You can either format one cell at a time by highlighting that specific cell, or you can format multiple cells at once by highlighting all of them and then choosing your formatting option. In some cases, you can also format specific text within a cell by clicking into a cell, selecting that text, and then choosing your formatting option.

There are basically four main ways to format cells or text in current versions of Excel.

First, you can use the Home tab and click on the option you want from there.

Second, you can use the Format Cells dialogue box. Either right-click from the main workspace and select the Format Cells option from the dropdown menu or use Ctrl + 1 to open the dialogue box.

Third, you can right-click from the main workspace and use the mini formatting menu that appears above or below the dropdown menu.

Finally, some of the most popular formatting options can be applied using control shortcuts. For example, Ctrl + B to bold text, Ctrl + I to apply italics, and Ctrl + U to apply a basic underline.

Okay, let's dive right in.

Align Text

By default, text within a cell is left-aligned and bottom-aligned. This won't be noticeable at the default row height and column width, but is definitely noticeable if you change either of those enough.

The easiest way to apply alignment to a cell is to go to the Alignment section on the Home tab. There are two rows of lines there on the left-hand side that visually show your choices. The top row contains Top, Middle, and Bottom alignment choices. The second row contains Left, Center, and Right. You can choose one option from each row.

In the screenshot below I've clicked on Cell B2 where I've chosen Middle Align and Center. You can see those options selected in the Alignment section of the Home tab.

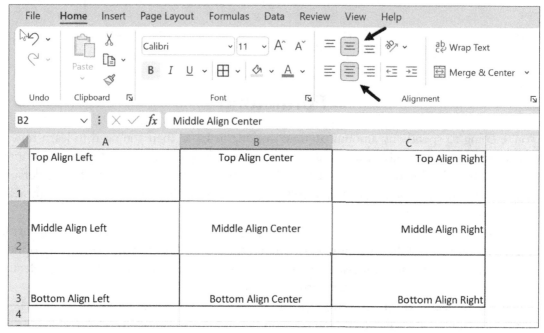

You can also see examples in Cells A1 through C3 in the screenshot above of all nine combinations.

The second-best choice for applying alignment is to use the Alignment tab of the Format Cells dialogue box. The Horizontal and Vertical alignment dropdown menus will give you the same choices as well as a few others that you're unlikely to use.

The mini formatting bar includes an option for centering your text, but that's the only alignment option it includes.

Angle Text

You can choose to angle your text in various ways using the dropdown menu under the angled "ab" with an arrow under it on the top row of the Alignment section of the Home tab.

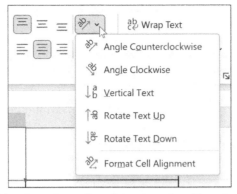

It has a handful of pre-defined options for changing the direction of text within a cell. You can choose Angle Counterclockwise, Angle Clockwise, Vertical Text, Rotate Text Up, and Rotate Text Down.

(It also offers another way to access the Alignment tab of the Format Cells dialogue box by clicking on Format Cell Alignment at the bottom of that dropdown menu.)

The Format Cells dialogue box lets you specify an exact degree for angling your text. So if you want to angle text at say a 30 degree angle, you'd need to do that in the Format Cells dialogue box. You can either enter that value in the Degrees field or click on a point in the Orientation box.

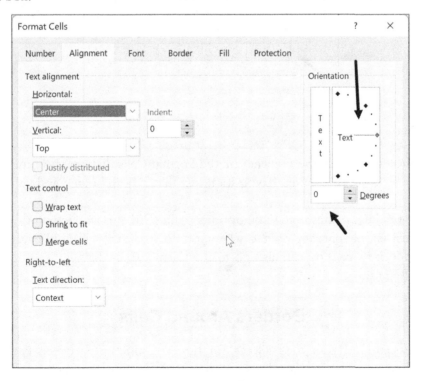

Bold Text

You can bold text in a number of ways. For each option below, select the text within a cell that you want to bold or the entire cell or cells first.

My default is to use Ctrl + B.

Another quick option is to click on the large capital B in the Font section of the Home tab.

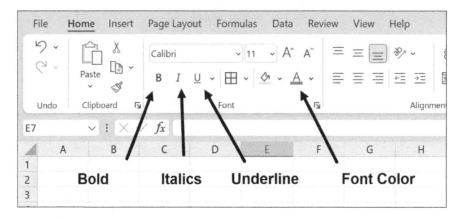

Or you can choose the capital B from the mini formatting toolbar.

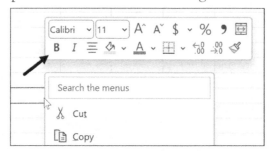

Your final option is to go to the Font tab of the Format Cells dialogue box and choose Bold from the Font Style options listing. If you want text that is both bolded and italicized, choose Bold Italic.

To remove bolding, you use the same options again (Ctrl + B or click on the capital B). If the selected text is only partially bolded when you do so, Excel will bold everything first so you'll have to do it twice. You can also go to the Format Cells dialogue box and change the Font Style to Regular.

Borders Around Cells

Placing borders around your data allows for better distinction between each cell and is something I do almost always when I create a data table. It's also very helpful when you print data from Excel, because that background grid that you see when working in Excel isn't actually present when you print.

Let me show you.

Here are those alignment choices pictured above as seen in Excel with no border around the individual cells. You can see that there is a faint line around each cell, right?

Here is the print preview of the first two columns of that image:

Note how the borders are no longer showing on the page? That's because the default cell borders that you see when working in Excel do not print. You have to add your own borders if you want your data to print with borders around it.

For the final comparison, this is that same information in print preview with a border added:

(Print preview, which we'll discuss in the chapter on how to print, is the best way to see how your data will actually appear when printed without wasting paper actually printing the document.)

There are three main ways to add borders around a cell or set of cells.

The easiest is also the newest.

If all you want is a simple basic border around a range of cells, go to the Font section on the Home tab and click on the dropdown arrow for the Borders dropdown option. It's a four-square grid with an arrow next to it that's located between the U used for underlining and the color bucket used for filling a cell with color.

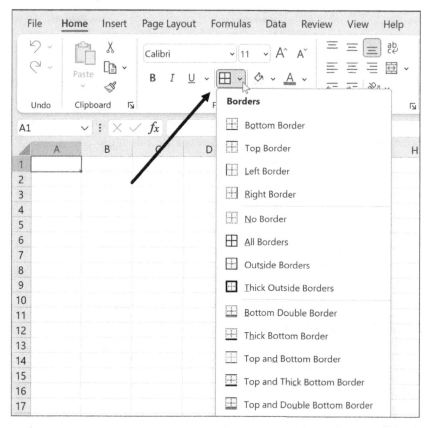

Go to the bottom of the dropdown menu and choose Draw Border Grid:

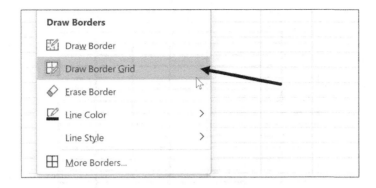

Click on it and then select the cells that you want to apply borders to.

Excel will apply the default line color and line style around all four edges of each cell you select. When you're done, use the Esc key to turn it off or click on the Border icon in the Font section of the Home tab.

For me, with the computer I'm working on and in Excel 365 as it exists in December 2022, the default line thickness isn't as dark as I would prefer it to be. I find myself wanting to change that line thickness to something I can see better on the screen.

But...

And here's where it gets weird, that line thickness is just fine in print preview. And when I choose the darker line that looks best to me on the screen, it's way too thick in print preview.

Now, I don't know if this is because of the computer I'm using which has better graphics than computers I've used in the past, or if this is part of the new streamlined appearance they rolled out with Office 2021.

But it's something to check on your own computer. Because if I were in an office environment where I was designing worksheets that others had to use and print, I'd need to be very careful that I didn't set the appearance of my worksheets to what I visually prefer since those settings will not print well.

Let me show you what I'm seeing. This is what the thick line option looks like on my worksheet:

	A	B	C	D	E	F	G	H
1								
2								
3								
4								
5								
6								
7								

Not bad, right? But this is what it looks like in print preview:

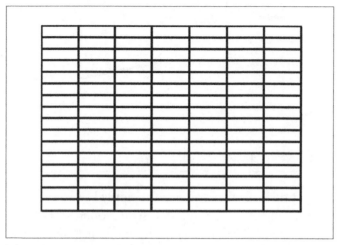

Horrible. That thick border is best for outlining a table, not for interior lines.

Which is all to say, if you're going to add borders to a document in Excel using Excel 2021 or Excel 365 and that document will be printed, be sure to look at that document in print preview before you print or provide it to others and adjust your borders accordingly.

Okay. Now, how do you adjust those lines from the default?

Go to the bottom of the Borders dropdown menu and choose one of the options from the Line Style secondary dropdown menu:

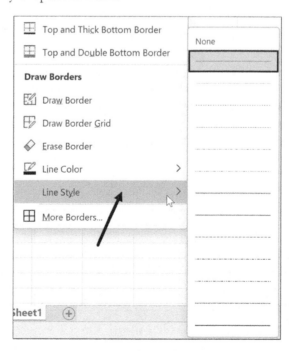

To change the line color, use the Line Color secondary dropdown menu.

The key, though, is that you need to change your line style or line color *before* you apply any borders to your cells.

That means since I don't like the default line style anymore that step one for me is to choose my line style from the dropdown. Step two is to then choose Draw Border Grid from the dropdown. Step three is to select the cells I want to add a border to. Step four is to hit Esc when I'm done.

Excel will keep that changed line style as the current default as long as that file is open.

If you have specific edges of cells where you want a border, you can use the Draw Border instead of the Draw Border Grid option. Simply select it and then click on the edge of a cell where you want to place a border line.

Draw Border when used on a range of cells at one time will apply a border around the perimeter of those selected cells but leave the inner cell borders alone.

So here, for example, I used Draw Border Grid with the default line style, highlighted my cells, and then changed the line style to the thickest option, chose Draw Border, and highlighted those exact same cells again.

That combination gave me a table with interior lines that were thin and a dark exterior border.

Be sure each time that you choose Draw Border Grid or Draw Border that you see a pencil shape before you start highlighting your cells. There were a few times I clicked on that option and it didn't turn into the pencil for me so didn't work.

Also, hit Esc when you're done to turn off that pencil.

That is the easiest way I think to draw a table in current versions of Excel. But there are a couple other ways to do it.

That same Border dropdown menu has a number of choices at the top that you can use. With those options, though, you first need to select the cells you want to format and then choose the option you want from the dropdown.

All Borders is one I've used often as well as Thick Outside Borders. But if you use both together like I could have to create the table in the screenshot above, be sure to apply them in the right order. All Borders first, Thick Outside Borders second.

The other option for applying borders is to select your cells and then go to the Border tab of the Format Cells dialogue box either by clicking on More Borders at the bottom of the borders dropdown menu or by right-clicking on the selected cells and choosing Format Cells from that dropdown. Here is that Border tab:

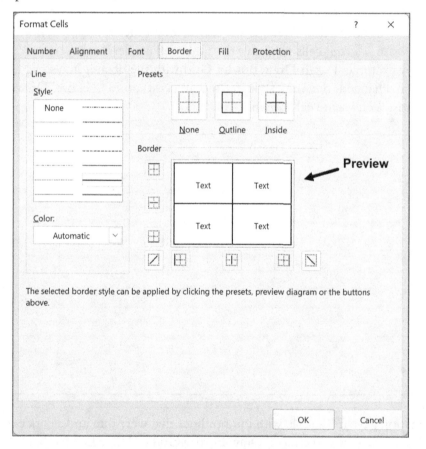

The image in the Border section of the dialogue box that shows four cells with Text in them, will show the current formatting for the selected cells.

To change that formatting, choose your line style and color on the left-hand side and then either click on the presets (none, outline, inside) above the preview or on the individual border thumbnails around the perimeter. You'll see the preview update as you click on each option.

The Format Cells dialogue box is the only way I know of to place a slanted line in a cell.

As I've done a few times in the examples above, you can combine different line styles and line colors in the same table. You just need to think through the order of applying them and make any color or line style choice first before trying to apply it to your entries.

Here is an example where I'm using three different line styles (thick, medium, and dotted line) as well as two line colors. Each of those had to be applied separately with changes to the style and/or color made before I chose the line position.

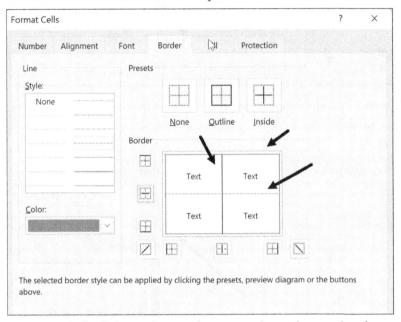

If you're in the Format Cells dialogue box and want to clear what you've done and start over, you can select None from the Presets section. The corresponding option in the dropdown menu is No Border. This does not, however, reset your line style and color choices, so if you changed those you'll need to manually change them back before you draw new borders in that worksheet. (Or close the worksheet and reopen it to reset to the default choices if you're not sure what they are.)

Color a Cell (Fill Color)

You can color (or fill) an entire cell with any color you want. I do this often when building tables. I will add fill color to the header rows of my tables and also to any columns that are either labels or non-input columns.

Like here with this example of the MAXIFS function where the header rows in each table have a green fill color, the cells with calculated results have a gray fill color, and the cells with the text of the formulas used have a blue fill color.

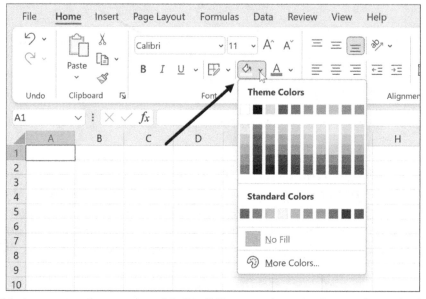

	A	B	C	D	E	F	G	H
1	Score	Teacher	Gender					
2	50	Smith	F					
3	49	Barker	M				F		M
4	68	Vasquez	F			98.00	Smith	94.00
5	75	Smith	M			90.00	Barker	93.00
6	90	Barker	F			68.00	Vasquez	76.00
7	94	Smith	M					
8	93	Barker	M		Cell F4:	=MAXIFS($A$2:$A$13,$B$2:$B$13,$G4,$C$2:$C$13,$F$3)
9	91	Smith	F		Cell H4:	=MAXIFS($A$2:$A$13,$B$2:$B$13,$G4,$C$2:$C$13,$H$3)
10	76	Vasquez	M					
11	82	Smith	F					
12	64	Barker	M					
13	98	Smith	F					
14								

To add fill color to a cell(s), highlight the cell(s) you want to color, go to the Font section of the Home tab, and click on the arrow to the right of the paint bucket that by default has a yellow line under it.

This should bring up a colors menu with 70 different colors to choose from, including many that are arranged as complementary themes. If you want one of those colors, just click on it.

(If you just wanted the default yellow color you could click on the paint bucket image without needing to bring up the dropdown menu. After you choose a color that option will change to show the last color used, so you can always click on the image to apply whatever color is shown without needing to use the dropdown menu.)

For more color options or to specify a specific color, click on More Colors at the bottom of the dropdown menu to bring up the Colors dialogue box.

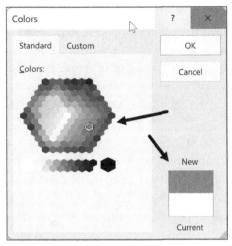 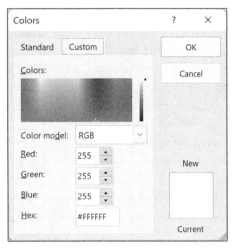

The first tab of that box, Standard, has a honeycomb-like image in the center that includes a number of colors you can choose from by clicking into the honeycomb. Shades of black, white, or gray can be selected just below that.

When you select a color it will show in the bottom right corner in the top half of the rectangle there under the heading New.

The second tab is the Custom tab. Click on it and you'll see a rectangle with a rainbow of colors that you can click on to select a color.

It also allows you to enter specific RGB, HSL, or Hex code values to get the exact color you need. (If you have a corporate color palette, for example, they should give you the values for each of the corporate colors. At least my employers always have.)

RGB is the default option, but you can change that in the dropdown menu.

Or you can enter a specific Hex code at the bottom if you have that.

On the Custom tab, you can also use the arrow on the right-hand side to darken or lighten your color.

If you like your choice, click on OK. If you don't want to add color to a cell after all, choose Cancel.

If you add Fill Color to a cell and later want to remove it, select the cell, go back to the dropdown menu, and choose the No Fill option.

Column Width

If your columns aren't the width you want, you have three options for adjusting them.

First, you can right-click on the column and choose Column Width from the dropdown menu. When the box showing you the current column width appears, enter a new column width. (I don't use this one often because I'm not a good judge of how wide I need to make a column in terms of a specific numeric value.)

Second, you can place your cursor to the right side of the column name—it should look like a line with arrows on either side when you have it in the right spot—and then left-click and drag either to the right or left until the column is as wide as you want it to be.

Or, third, you can place your cursor on the right side of the column name and double left-click. This will make the column as wide or as narrow as the widest text currently in that column. (Usually. Sometimes this one has a mind of its own. But it almost always works with shorter text entries.)

To adjust all column widths in your document at once, you can highlight the entire worksheet (Ctrl + A or click in the top left corner) and then apply one of the above options. A double-left click on any column border will adjust each column to the contents in that column. (Usually. See comment above.) Manually adjusting the width of one column or setting a Column Width using the dropdown menu, will apply that width to all columns in the worksheet.

Currency Formatting

Currency has two main formatting options, Currency and Accounting, but there are a number of other choices available as well.

To format cells using one of the currency options, highlight the cell(s) you want formatted, and then go to the Number section of the Home tab, and either click on the $ sign (which will use the Accounting format) or click on the dropdown arrow for General and choose Currency or Accounting.

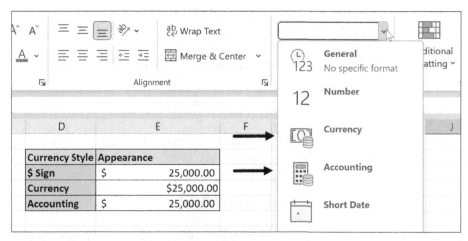

As you can see in the image above, the main difference between the two options is where they place the $ sign relative to the numbers. The Currency option places the $ sign right next to the number, the Accounting option left-aligns the $ sign and right-aligns the numbers.

The $ sign option in the Number section of the Home tab has a dropdown menu where you can choose other common currencies. Also, if you just want your currency to display as whole numbers you can click on the Decrease Decimal option twice, which is located in that same row.

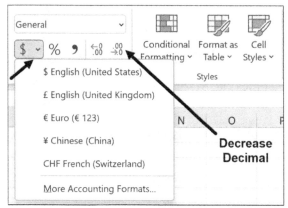

If those options aren't enough for you, you can go to the Number tab of the Format Cells dialogue box and then either use the Currency or Accounting category:

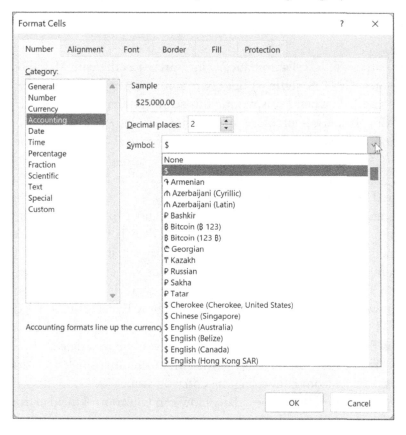

That gives a much larger range of currencies to choose from. The Currency category also includes multiple choices for how to distinguish negative values.

You can also use Ctrl + Shift + $ to apply the Currency format to a selected cell or range of cells.

Date Formatting

Not only does Excel sometimes like to format things as a date that aren't but it also sometimes has a mind of its own about how to format dates. Here are a few examples:

Input Value	Excel Default Displayed Result	Excel Short Date
3/6	6-Mar	3/6/2022
January	January	January
January 2020	Jan-20	1/1/2020
3/6/20	3/6/2020	3/6/2020

In the first column you can see the text I entered. In the second column you can see what Excel did with that text. The third column is the date, when applicable, that Excel assigned to what I'd entered.

So that first entry 3/6, Excel automatically interpreted as the date March 6th (for me, here in the United States with U.S. settings) but rewrote it as 6-Mar and added the current year to the date, which was 2022 when I was writing this so stored that date as March 6, 2022.

The second one, January, it left alone and did not turn into a date.

The third, January 2020, it converted into a date, rewrote as Jan-20, and stored as January 1, 2020.

The fourth, 3/6/20, it reformatted slightly, and treated as March 6, 2020. (Again, for me, here in the United States where month is written first.)

This demonstrates a key thing you need to remember about Excel and dates. It will always insist on having a month, day of the month, and year for every date. If you don't provide that, Excel will do it for you. And it is over-eager to turn anything that may possibly be a date into a date.

The other thing to know is that once Excel decides something is a date, you can't really change that with formatting. So with that first entry there I tried to change that to a Text format and it showed it as the number 44626 which is how Excel really stores dates behind the scenes. (As the 44,626th day since Excel's start date.)

Which means that if Excel ever turns an entry of yours into a date and you didn't want it to, the best thing is to Undo and then retype the entry using that single apostrophe at the start of the cell to keep Excel from converting the entry on you.

But let's say you did want that to be a date. How can you control the date format that Excel applies to your date?

Click on the cell with your date in it, go to the Number section of the Home tab, click on the dropdown menu which should show General by default, and then choose either Short Date or Long Date from there. You will be able to see examples of what that date will look like when chosen:

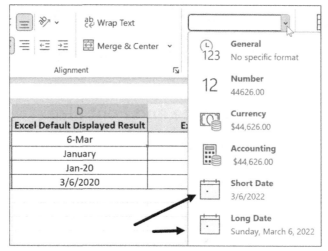

Usually, Short Date will be the one you want.

But if neither of those work for you, go to the Number tab of the Format Cells dialogue box, and click on the Date category. There will be about a dozen options to choose from there.

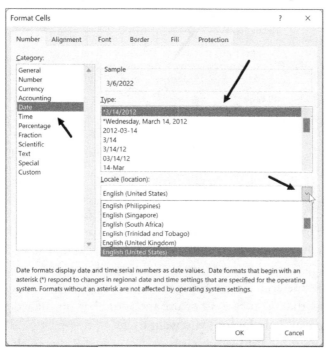

Note that there is also a Locale dropdown menu that lets you choose formats used in other countries. For example, here in the United States 3/6 is March 6th, but in many other parts of the world 3/6 is June 3rd, so if you're going to use that Short Date format understand that it is a regional format that may be misinterpreted by others on a printed document. (I believe Excel adjusts the display for the local country settings, so it won't be an issue when looking at the Excel file, but be careful there just in case.)

You can also use Ctrl + Shift + # to apply a date format that uses day, month, and year. For me the format was 2-Jan-20 for January 2, 2020.

Font Choice and Font Size

The current default font choice in Excel is Calibri and the default font size is 11 point.

You may have strong preferences about what font you use or work for a company that uses specific fonts for its brand or just want some variety in terms of font size or type within a specific document. In that case, you will need to change those settings.

There are a few ways to do this. Each requires selecting your text or cells first.

Once you've done that, option one is to go to the Font section on the Home tab and select a different font or font size from the dropdown menus there by clicking on the one you want.

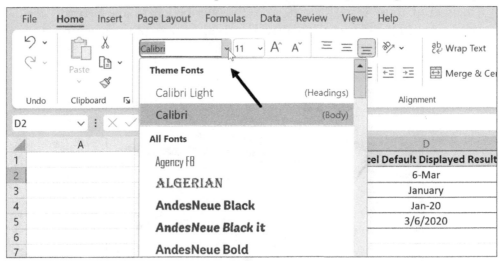

Which fonts are available in the font dropdown will depend on which fonts you have on your computer. Most people have a number of fonts already available. I have a large number of additional fonts so you may see different fonts listed there than I do.

Excel shows your theme font at the top and then the rest of your fonts are shown in alphabetical order below that. You can either use the scroll bar on the side to scroll down or you can start typing the name of the font you want to get to that part of the list.

Each font will display in the list using that font. You can see this in the screenshot above where Agency is a very different font from Andes Neue and Algerian.

The font size dropdown only has the most common sizes listed. It lists 8, 9, 10, 11, and 12 pt but then starts jumping up in numbers. If you have a specific font size you want that isn't listed, you can just type it in.

You also have the option to increase or decrease the font one listed size at a time by clicking on the A's with little arrows that are shown next to the font dropdown box. The bigger of the two, on the left, increases the font size. The smaller one decreases the font size.

All of these options are also available in the mini formatting menu if you right-click in the main workspace after selecting your cells.

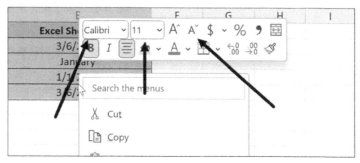

Your other option, which really doesn't give you any additional functionality, is to use the Font tab of the Format Cells dialogue box.

Font Color

The default color for all text in Excel is black, but you can change that if you want or need to. (For example, if you've filled a cell with a darker color you may want to change the font color to white to make the text in that cell more visible.)

You have three options. All require selecting the text or cells first.

After that, the first option is to go to the Font section on the Home tab and click on the arrow next to the A that by default will have a red line under it. (Or click on the A if you want the color shown.)

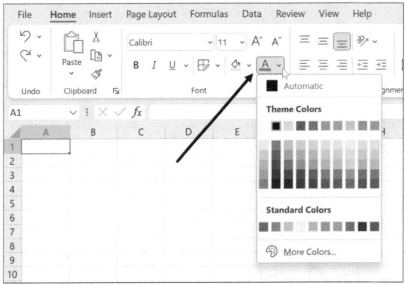

You can then choose from one of the 70 colors that are listed, and if those aren't enough of a choice you can click on More Colors and select your color from the Colors dialogue box. (See Coloring a Cell for more detail about that option.)

Second, you can use the mini formatting menu.

Third, you can use the Color dropdown in the Font tab of the Format Cells dialogue box.

Indent Text

If you want your text within your cell to be indented from the edge of the cell, you can increase the indent to make that happen by selecting the cell, going to the Alignment section of the Home tab, and clicking on the Increase Indent option that's located to the left of the Merge & Center option.

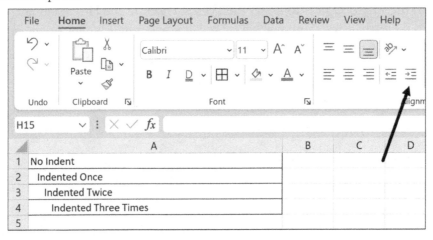

You can see how that would impact text placement in the screenshot above.

To decrease the indent, use the Decrease Indent option located to the left of the Increase Indent option.

You can also use the Indent field in the Alignment section of the Format Cells dialogue box. It will accept a whole number for the number of times to indent the text.

Italicize Text

To italicize text, highlight the text selection or cells containing text you want to italicize, and then use Ctrl + I or click on the slanted I in the Font section on the Home tab or in the mini formatting menu.

You can also change the Font Style option in the Font tab of the Format Cells dialogue box to Italic or Bold Italic.

To remove italics from text or cells that already have it, select that text and then use Ctrl + I or click on the slanted I in the Font section of the Home tab or the mini formatting menu. You may have to do this twice if you select text that is only partially italicized since Excel will apply italics to the entire selection first.

You can also remove italics by changing the Font Style back to Regular in the Format Cells dialogue box.

Merge & Center

Merge and Center is a specialized command that can come in handy when you're working with a table where you want a header that spans multiple columns of data. (Don't use it if you plan to do a lot of data analysis with what you've input into the worksheet because it will mess with your ability to filter, sort, or use pivot tables. It's really for creating a finalized, pretty-looking report.)

What it does is merges the cells you select and then centers your text across those merged cells.

You can merge cells across columns and down rows. So you could, for example, merge four cells that span two columns and two rows into one big cell while keeping all of the other cells in those columns and rows separate. But what I usually am doing is just merging X number of cells in a single row.

If you're going to merge and center cells that contain text, make sure that the text you want to keep is in the top-most and left-most of the cells you plan to merge and center. Data in the other cells that are being merged will be deleted. (You'll get a warning message to this effect if you have values in any of the other cells.)

To use this option, first select all of the cells you want to merge.

Next, go to the Alignment section of the Home tab and choose Merge & Center. This will combine your selected cells into one cell and center the contents from that left-uppermost cell across the selection.

Like so:

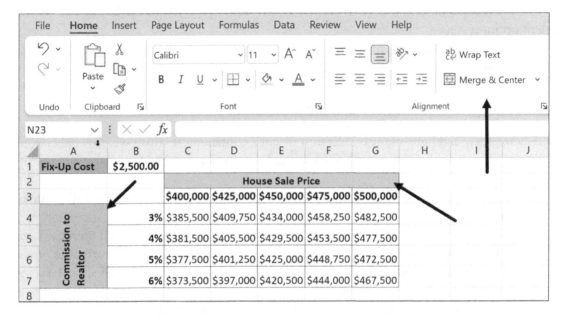

In the screenshot above I've merged and centered the text "House Sale Price" across Columns C through G in Row 2. I've also merged and centered the text "Commission to Realtor" across Rows 4 through 7 in Column A. (You'll note that I also changed the alignment of the commission text.)

That is the option I use most often, but there are additional choices available if you click on the dropdown arrow for Merge & Center. You can also choose to Merge Across (which will merge the cells in each row of the selected range separately and will not center the text) or to Merge Cells (which will merge all of the selected cells but won't center the text).

If you ever need to unmerge merged cells you can do so by selecting those cells and then clicking on the Unmerge Cells option from that dropdown.

You can also merge or unmerge cells by using the Merge Cells checkbox in the Alignment tab of the Format Cells dialogue box.

Merge & Center is also an option in the mini formatting menu. It's located in the top right corner of the menu. Clicking on it for previously merged cells will unmerge those cells.

Number Formatting

In addition to date and currency formatting, which we already discussed, you can apply other basic number formatting to your cells.

The first option is to use the Number section of the Home tab. The second option is to use the mini formatting menu. And the final option is to use the Format Cells dialogue box.

There are three default number styles in the dropdown menu on the Home tab that you may want to consider. If you already have values entered, the dropdown menu will show you a sample of how each one will look.

Here, for example, I used 10000 as my entry and you can see how General, Number, and Scientific would display that number:

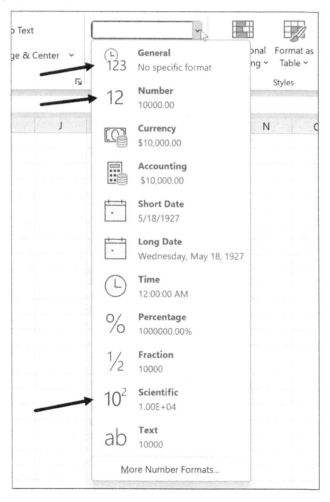

I often prefer to use the Comma Style option that's available below the dropdown and is just shown as a big comma because that one includes a comma for thousands where Number does not:

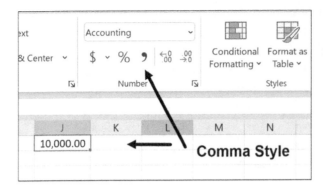

It is also available in the mini formatting menu.

Ctrl + Shift + exclamation mark (!) will give a similar but not identical result to the Comma Style option. (The spacing within the cell is different.)

And, as with all other number formatting options, there is a more detailed option in the Number section of the Format Cells dialogue box, in this case using the Number category.

You can also use the Increase and Decrease Decimal options in the Number section of the Home tab or in the mini formatting menu to change the number of decimal places for your values, just be sure to do that after you've applied your number format, not before.

Percent Formatting

To format numbers as a percentage, your first option is to highlight the cell(s), and click on the percent sign in the Number section of the Home tab or the mini formatting menu. This will convert the value to a percent with no decimal places.

Your second option is to use the dropdown menu in the Number section of the Home tab and choose Percentage from there. This will format the value as a percentage, but also include two decimal places.

Your final option is to use the Percentage category in the Number tab of the Format Cells dialogue box which will let you specify the number of decimal places to use.

With any of the above options, be sure that your numbers are formatted correctly or it won't work properly. In other words, 0.5 will translate to 50% but 50 will translate to 5000% so you want your entries pre-formatting to be .5 not 50 if you're looking for 50%.

(You can fix this by dividing those entries by 100, copying that result, and then pasting special values over the original values.)

Row Height

If your rows aren't the correct height, you have three options for adjusting them.

First, you can right-click on the row you want to adjust, choose Row Height from the dropdown menu, and when the box showing you the current row height appears, enter a new row height.

Second, you can place your cursor along the lower border of the row number for the row you want to adjust until it looks like a line with arrows above and below. Left-click and hold while you move the cursor up or down until the row is as tall as you want it to be.

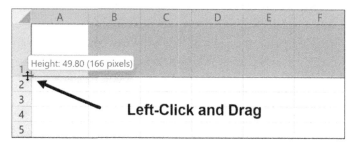

Third, you can place your cursor along the lower border of the row, and double left-click. This will fit the row height to the text in the cell. (Usually. Sometimes in the past it would not work with really large amounts of text and the only option was to manually resize the row height.)

To adjust all row heights in your document at once, highlight the entire worksheet (Ctrl + A or click in the top left corner) first and then use one of the options above. Entering a specific row height or clicking and dragging will keep all rows the same height. Double-left-clicking will resize each row to its contents. (Theoretically.)

Underline Text

Underlining text works much the same way that bolding and italics work.

For a basic single-line underline select the text or cells with text that you want to underline and then use Ctrl + U or click on the underlined U in the Font section of the Home tab.

You can also use the Underline dropdown in the Font section of the Format Cells dialogue box.

There are other underline types such as a double underline. For that, use the dropdown arrow next to the underlined U in the Font section of the Home tab or choose one of the options in the Format Cells dialogue box which includes single accounting and double accounting options as well.

To remove underlining from text or cells that already have it, highlight the text and then use one of the above options again. If you applied a special underline type, then using Ctrl + U or clicking on the underlined U in the Font section will first change the underline to a single underline, so you have to do it twice to completely remove the underline.

Wrap Text

Wrap text is an essential one to learn if you want to use text in your worksheet and be able to see all of the text in that worksheet without expanding the width of your columns to make that happen.

To Wrap Text in a cell, select the cell(s), go to the Alignment section of the Home Tab, and click on the Wrap Text option in the top row.

Or you can go to the Alignment tab in the Format Cells dialogue box and check the box for Wrap Text in the Text Control section.

Here is an example of a FINRA regulation in the left-most column and then an analysis column next to it. The content of the cells in Rows 1 through 3 are the same as those in Rows 6 through 8. In Column A, Rows 2 and 3 did not wrap the text but Rows 7 and 8 did.

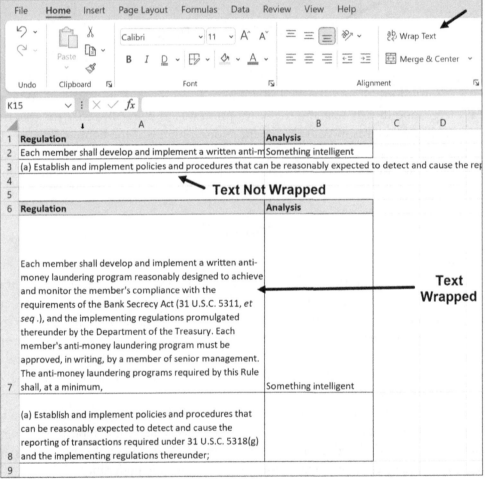

Note a few things. In the example at the top where the text is not wrapped, the text stops at the next column when there is content in that next column. You can see that in Cell A2. But when there isn't text in that next column, the text is visible on the screen. You can see that in Cell A3.

But when text is wrapped, like in Cells A7 and A8, the text moves to a new line when it reaches the border with the next column and as long as the row height is high enough, you can see the full text in that cell, regardless of what text may or may not be in any other column.

It also just looks much better when it's contained to the cell it belongs to.

(Excel does seem to have a maximum row height which will limit the amount of text you can display in one cell, so if you have any cells with lots of text in them, check to make sure that the full contents of the cell are actually visible. You may have to manually adjust the row height or it just may not be possible to see all of the text.)

* * *

Okay. That was our alphabetical discussion of the various formatting options, but before we move on to sorting and filtering, I wanted to cover a couple more formatting tricks.

Copy Formatting From One Cell To Another

I find this one incredibly useful, although I use it more in Word than in Excel.

If you already have a cell formatted the way you want it, you can use the Format Painter located in the Clipboard section of the Home tab to sweep the formatting from that cell to other cells you want formatted the same way.

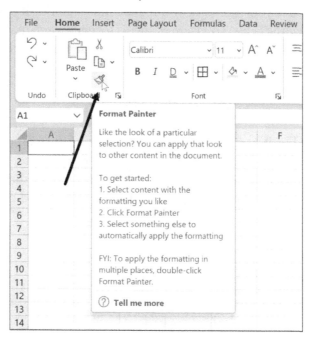

The help text sort of says it all.

First, select the cell(s) that have the formatting you want to copy (if the formatting is identical, just highlight one cell).

Next, click on the Format Painter. Double-click if you have more than one place you want to apply that formatting.

Finally, click into the cell(s) you want to copy the formatting to.

The contents in the destination cell will remain the same, but the font, font color, font size, cell borders, italics/bolding/underlining, and text alignment and orientation will all change to match that of the cell that you swept the formatting from.

If you double-clicked, use Esc or click on the Format Painter again to turn it off when you're done.

You can also find the Format Painter tool in the mini formatting menu.

You need to be careful using the Format Painter because it will change all formatting in your destination cells. So, if the cell you're copying the formatting from is bolded and has red text, both of those attributes will copy over even if all you were trying to do was copy the bold formatting. (This is more of a problem when using the tool in Word than in Excel, but it's still something to watch out for especially if you have borders around cells.)

Also, the tool copies formatting to whatever cell you select next, which can be a problem if the cell you're copying from isn't next to the one you're copying to. DO NOT use arrow keys to navigate between the cells. You need to click directly on the cell you're transferring the formatting to.

Remember, Ctrl + Z is your friend if you make a mistake. But if you format sweep and then undo, you'll see that the cell(s) you were trying to format from are surrounded by a dotted border as if you had copied the cells. Be sure to hit the Esc key before you continue to turn that off.

Clear Formatting

I don't use this often, but it can be handy if I had a lot of formatting in a worksheet and deleted the contents but the formatting is still there and I don't want it anymore.

To clear formatting, select the cells where you want to do this (or the entire worksheet with Ctrl + A), and then go to the Editing section of the Home tab and click on the dropdown arrow under Clear.

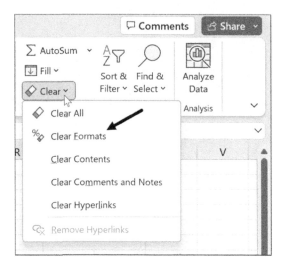

The Clear Formats option will remove all formatting from the selected cells. Clear All will remove contents and formatting at the same time.

* * *

Okay, that was formatting. We have three more topics to go: Sorting, Filtering, and Printing. And then we're done with this introduction. Yay. The end is in sight.

Sorting and Filtering

Two of the most common and basic ways I analyze or use data in Excel is by sorting or filtering. (The other option I use frequently is PivotTables, which are covered in the next book in this series.)

Sorting

Sorting allows you to display your information in a specific order. For example, by date, value, or alphabetically. You can also sort across multiple columns, so you can, for example, sort first by date, then by name, then by amount.

To sort your data, select the data, including your header row if there is one, and all columns of related information.

And do be sure that you select *all* columns of your data. Because this is one of those areas where if you choose the first five columns out of ten and sort those five, there's no way to return things to an order that matches those five columns that were sorted with the ones that weren't.

So you have to be a little careful here because sorting is one of the ways to irretrievably break a data set.

If you set your data up with the first row as the header and all of the rest as data with no subtotals or grand totals, the best thing to do is just use Ctrl + A or click in the top left corner of your worksheet to select all of the cells in the worksheet. Excel will then figure out the limits of your data from there.

If you have a table of data that starts lower down on the page or that has a summary row or that is followed by other data, be sure to only select the cells in the data set that you want to sort, because Excel will sort everything you select whether it makes sense to do so or not.

(I often mess this up and end up sorting my data so that my summary row is included, for example, so instead of seeing my best-selling title at the top I see a value for all sales of all books instead. It's not the end of the world if that happens, but it is mildly annoying and something to fix before anyone else sees your data.)

Once you've selected your data, go to the Editing section of the Home tab. Click on the arrow next to Sort & Filter, and choose Custom Sort.

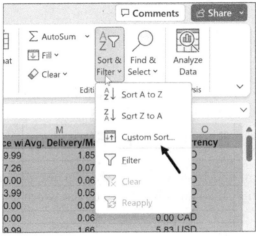

(The Sort A to Z and Sort Z to A options are ones I try not to use simply because that gives a little too much control to Excel about how it sorts the data. It seems to default to sorting by values in the first column when you choose that option, but I'm not always clear on where it goes from there and I've had it not work for me. Also, I often am not interested in sorting by the first column, so I just default to Custom Sort from the beginning. Less thought required.)

You can also go to the Sort & Filter section of the Data tab and click on the Sort option there. That's the one I tend to use.

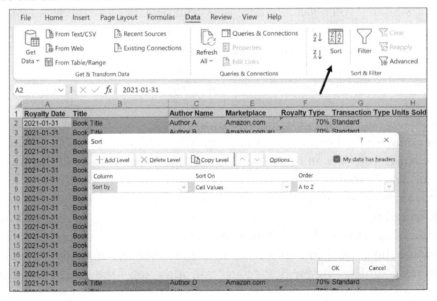

Either option will open the Sort dialogue box that you can see in the screenshot above.

The first thing you need to do is tell Excel whether or not your data has headers. It will guess the answer, but review to make sure it got it right.

If your data does have headers that box in the top corner that says, "My data has headers" should be checked.

If you indicate that there is a header row, it will not be included in your sort and will remain the first row of your data. Also, the Sort By dropdown will use the text in that first row for the dropdown menu choices. Like so:

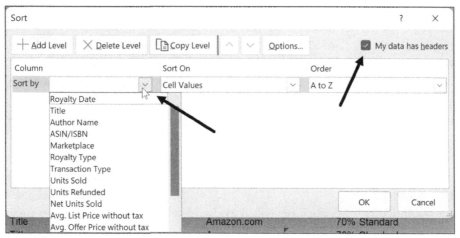

If you don't have a header row, the listed field name choices for Sort By will be the generic column names (Column A, Column B, etc.) and all of your selected data will be sorted, including the first row. Which makes sense to have happen if, for example, you are sorting a subset of your data.

When might you do this?

I have a worksheet that tracks my advertising spend where I need to do this because when I input the advertising spend I just do it in the order it's shown on my reports. However, when I'm matching that spend up to sales to see if my ads were profitable it's easier to do that if I sort alphabetically by title. But I only want to do that for the current month. That worksheet tracks advertising spend back to 2013. I only select the rows for the current month and then sort by title.

So it can happen that you don't have a header row to include for your sort.

The next step is to choose your sort order.

Decide what the primary criteria you want to sort by is and then choose that column from the Sort By dropdown menu.

After you've done that, choose what to sort on for that sort option. For a basic sort, like mine above where I want to sort by title, you'll generally leave this alone because you want to sort by the values in each cell.

There are also options to sort by cell color, font color, and conditional formatting icon which will only be useful to you if you've manually applied color to certain entries or used conditional formatting to do so. (Conditional formatting is covered in the next book in this series.)

Finally, you have to specify the Order that will be used for your sort. The choices there are going to depend on the type of data.

For text use A to Z to sort alphabetical or Z to A to sort reverse alphabetical. I also sometimes use the Custom List option when I have a column with the months of the year or the days of the week in it because Excel already has those set up.

For numbers it's Smallest to Largest or Largest to Smallest.

For dates it's Oldest to Newest or Newest to Oldest.

The default choices are A to Z, Smallest to Largest, and Oldest to Newest. But if you want to use a different option you can change this using the dropdown arrow.

If all you want is to sort by one column, then you're done. Click OK and Excel will sort your data.

If you want to then sort by another column, you need to add that second column to the Sort dialogue box.

(For example, maybe you sort first by year, then month, then Customer so that all of the sales for a particular month are grouped together and then within that month the information is sorted by customer name.)

To add a second sort level, click on Add Level and select your next column to sort by and your criteria for that sort.

Here for example, I have four total sort levels:

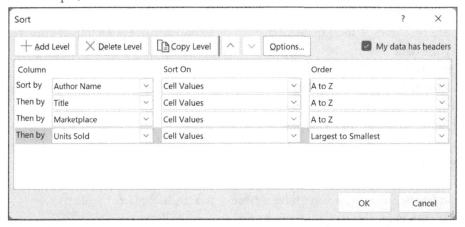

The data will first be sorted by author name, then by title, then by marketplace, and finally by units sold in reverse order from largest to smallest.

If you add a level you don't need, like I just did here with units sold which should only have one value per marketplace, title, and author, click on it and then choose Delete Level from the top of the dialogue box.

Also, if you have multiple levels but decide that they should be sorted in a different order, you can use the arrows at the top to move the selected sort level up or down.

The default for sort is to sort top to bottom, so down a column, but you can click on Options to sort left to right or to make your sort case-sensitive. (Something I rarely need, but have used once or twice.)

If you change your mind about sorting your data, click Cancel or the X in the top right corner of the dialogue box. Otherwise, when you're done with your sort options, click OK and Excel will sort your data.

If you get a sort that has a mistake in it, use Ctrl + Z to undo and try again. Don't try to fix a bad sort, just undo it and start over.

Filtering

The other thing I do often is filter my data. Sometimes I just want to look at a quick subset of a data table. For example, all of the sales for Author A. The data in the table is just fine, I don't need to summarize it in any way, I just want the rest of the entries hidden while I look at that subset.

Filtering allows you to do that as long as your data is set up the right way. (Ideally, a header row at the top, rows of data below, no subtotals or blank lines or blank columns.)

To turn on filtering for your data table, the first step is to click on any cell in the first row of the table and then go to the Editing section of the Home tab, click on the arrow next to Sort & Filter, and choose Filter.

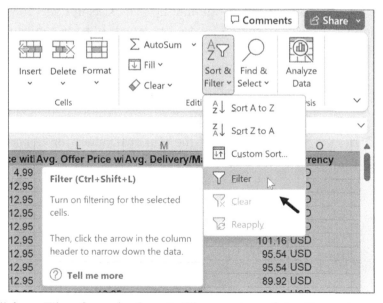

You can also click on Filter from the Sort & Filter section of the Data tab.

(It's possible that Excel will now appropriately apply filtering as long as you've clicked on any cell in the data table or selected the whole worksheet even if you don't click in a cell in the first row of the data table, but in older versions of Excel this could be an issue so I still as a best practice try to click on a cell in the header row before I apply filtering.)

Once filtering has been applied, you should see little arrows in the bottom right corner of each cell in that first row of the data table. If there was a gap in the columns in the table, only the columns on that side of the table will have the filter option. Like here:

F	G	H	I	J	K	L
Royalty Typ ▾	Transaction Ty ▾	Units Sold ▾			Avg. List Price wit	Avg. Offer Price wi
70%	Free - Price Match	65			4.99	0.00
60%	Standard - Paperba	21			12.95	12.95
60%	Standard - Paperba	21			12.95	12.95
60%	Standard - Paperba	19			12.95	12.95
60%	Standard - Paperba	18			12.95	12.95
60%	Standard - Paperba	18			12.95	12.95

I clicked into Cell H1 before I turned on filtering. So all of the columns on that side of the gap have a filter option now. But see that Cells K1 and L1 do not, because Excel doesn't see them as part of the same data table due to that gap.

You can overcome this by selecting the entire worksheet before you apply filtering. If you do that, Excel will apply a filter option to every column in that first row, up to the point where the last column with text is.

From here on out, I'm going to talk about filtering as it exists in Excel 365 as of December 2022. This is one of those areas where you need to watch out for compatibility with older Excel versions. If you are working with someone who has an older version of Excel, I highly recommend that you never share with them a file that has filtering already applied, because there are types of filtering you can do now that you could not do in the past.

Okay, then.

If you click on the arrow for any given column, you should see a list of all potential values in that column. Here, for example, are all of the potential values for Column C in this data table, which contains author names.

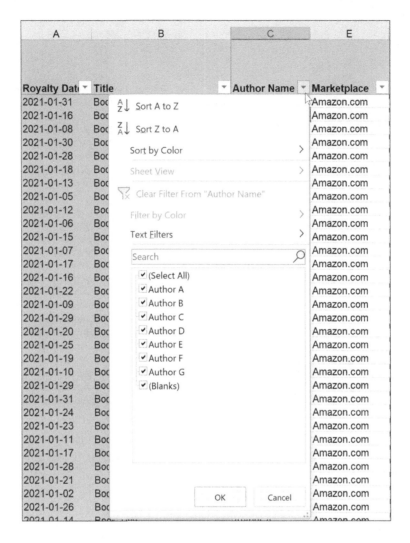

Note that there are checkboxes next to each value and that by default they are all checked.

For really long data sets (tens of thousands of rows) that have a lot of potential values this may not be a complete listing. (It definitely wasn't in older versions of Excel.)

If there are any values you don't want displayed, you can simply uncheck the box next to that value. Usually I want just one out of that list or maybe a few. The easiest way to accomplish this is to click on the box next to Select All. That removes all of the checks for all of the entries. You can then go through and check the boxes for the ones you want to see.

Like here where I now am only going to see results for Author A:

If the list of potential values is really long, you can start to type the name of the value you want to filter by into the Search field to make it appear within the visible list of entries.

Another option is to use filter criteria to narrow down what information is displayed. Depending on the type of data you're filtering and how it's formatted, the option will say Number Filters, Text Filters, Date Filters, etc. In the image above the filter option is Text Filters. It's located directly above the Search field.

Click on the arrow next to the filter name to open a secondary dropdown menu with available choices.

You should see options like "Equals" or "Does Not Equal" or "Begins With" or "Between" etc. The options differ depending on the type of data.

You can use these filter criteria to select only the rows where those criteria are met. So, for example, if I only want to see entries where the number of units sold is greater than 5, I can choose the Greater Than option under Number Filters in the Units Sold column.

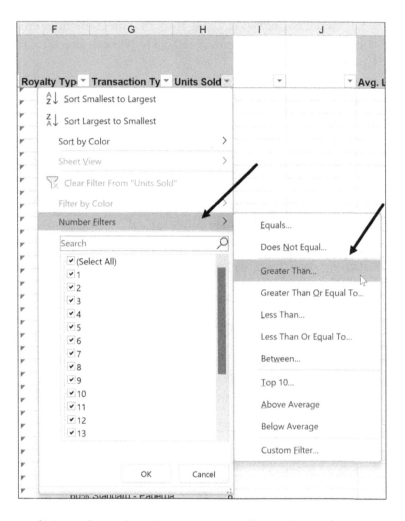

That brings up a dialogue box where I can enter my filter value and then click OK.

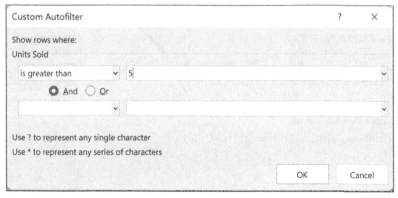

My data will now be filtered to only show those rows that meet the filter criteria I specified.

If you've color-coded cells using font color or cell color, you can also filter by those criteria, using the Filter by Color option.

When cells in your worksheet are filtered, the row numbers in your worksheet will be colored blue or aqua (depending on your theme settings), and you'll see that the row numbers skip since some rows are hidden.

For example, in the screenshot above Rows 2, 4, and 6 have been filtered out. The numbers for Rows 3, 5, 7, etc. are blue.

Columns where filtering is in place will show a funnel instead of an arrow in the corner of the header row like you can see above for Royalty Date and Author Name.

To remove filtering from a specific column, click on that filter image, and select Clear Filter from [Column Name].

To remove all filtering in a worksheet, go to the Editing section of the Home tab, click on Sort & Filter, and then choose Clear.

To turn off filtering entirely, click on the Filter option in that dropdown once more.

Printing

Alright, so that was the basics of how to work with your data within Excel. But there are going to be times when you want to print your results. Excel can be especially problematic that way, simply because what looks good on the screen doesn't always print well.

Basic printing in Excel is as simple as going to File, Print, (or using Ctrl + P) and then clicking on the Print icon. But don't do that. Take a moment before you do that to check all of your settings and look at your print preview first.

Here is what the Print screen looks like:

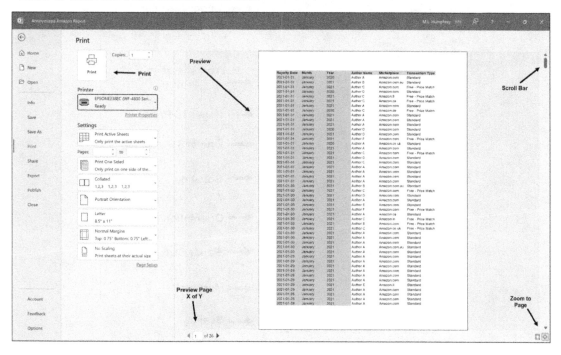

The image of a printer on the top under Print is what you ultimately will click on to print your document.

The preview in the right-hand side of the screen shows you what that document will look like when printed, page-by-page. You can see here how the first page of this document would look if I were to print it right now.

Down below that you can see what page this is and how many total pages will print. There are arrows there for moving between pages. You can also use the scroll bar on the right-hand side to move to the other pages.

In the bottom right corner are options to show margins and zoom to page. Zoom to Page can be useful if you can't read text or see what's on the page well and want to zoom in a bit. But generally I leave those alone.

Now let's look at the print options on the left-hand side:

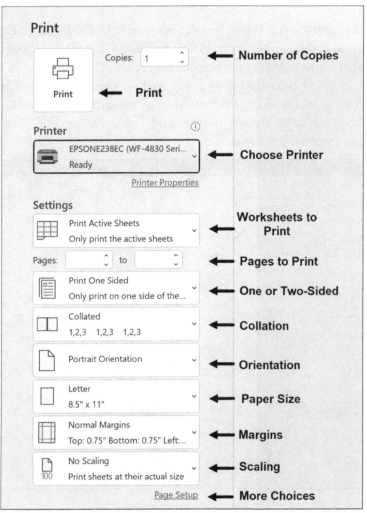

Print

Once you're ready to print your page, you can click on the button on the top left with the image of a printer that says Print to print your document.

Number of Copies

The Copies field is located to the right of the Print button. If you want to print more than one copy, change your number of copies in the Copies field using the up and down arrows or click into the field and type the desired number of copies.

Printer

This should display your computer's default printer, but if you want to use a different printer than that one or print to a PDF, click on the arrow next to the printer name and choose from the listed options. If the printer you want isn't listed, choose Add Printer from the dropdown menu and add the printer.

You generally won't need to click on that Printer Properties link that you can see below the dropdown.

Print Active Sheets / Print Entire Workbook / Print Selection

My version of Excel defaults to Print Active Sheets. This will generally be the worksheet you were working in when you chose to print.

However, you can select more than one worksheet by holding down the Control key and then clicking on another worksheet's name. When you do this, you'll see that the names of all of your selected worksheets are highlighted, not just one of them.

You can also right-click on a worksheet and choose Select All Sheets to select all of the worksheets in your workbook at once. (Be careful doing this because an edit to one worksheet will be an edit to all of them.)

I would only print multiple worksheets together if you're satisfied that each one is formatted the way you want it formatted already.

Also, choosing to print more than one sheet at a time either with Print Active Sheets or Print Entire Workbook, results in strange things happening to your headers and footers if you use those. For example, your page numbering will be across worksheets.

If you mean each worksheet to be a standalone report with numbered pages specific to that report, then you need to print each worksheet separately.

As I just alluded to, the Print Entire Workbook option prints all of the worksheets in your workbook.

Print Selection allows you to just print a highlighted section of a worksheet.

(Or worksheets. I happened to have three worksheets selected at once and when I highlighted the first twenty cells in one of those worksheets, the selection it was ready to print was those twenty cells in each of the three worksheets. So again, be careful that that makes sense to do.)

The dropdown also has an Ignore Print Area option which you could use if a worksheet has a print area set and you want to print everything on the worksheet not just the print area. (A print area lets you permanently specify which cells in a worksheet should be printed instead of the default of all cells with data in that worksheet.)

Pages

Just below the Print Active Sheets section is a row that says Pages and has two boxes with arrows at the side. Using this section, you can choose to just print a specific page or a subset of pages rather than the entire worksheet. To figure out which page(s) to print, look at the print preview.

For a single page use the same page number in both boxes. For a range of pages, put the first page of the range in the first box and the last page of the range in the second box.

In Excel you can only do a range of pages unlike Word where you can print a series of non-adjacent pages.

Changing the values in this section will NOT update your print preview.

Print One Sided / Print on Both Sides (long edge) / Print on Both Sides (short edge)

This option will only be available if you have a printer chosen that can do this.

The default is to just print on one side of the page. If you have a printer that can print on both sides of the page you can change your settings to do so either on the long edge or the short edge.

You generally will want the long edge option if your layout is going to be portrait style and the short edge option if your layout is going to be landscape style. (See below.)

Collated / Uncollated

This only matters if what you're printing has more than one page and if you're printing more than one copy.

In that case, you need to decide if you want to print one full copy at a time, x number of times, or if you want to print x copies of page 1 and then x copies of page 2 and then x copies of page 3 and so on until you've printed all pages of your document.

In general, I would choose collated, which is also the default, which prints one full copy at a time.

Portrait Orientation / Landscape Orientation

You can choose to print in either portrait orientation (with the short edge of the page on top) or landscape orientation (with the long edge of the page on top). You can see the difference in what will print on each page by changing the option in Excel and looking at your print preview.

Which option you choose will depend mostly on how many columns of data you have.

Assuming I'm dealing with a normal worksheet with rows of data across various columns, my goal is to fit all of my columns on one page if possible.

Sometimes changing the layout to landscape allows me to do that because it allows me to have more columns per page than I'd be able to fit in portrait mode.

If I have just a few columns of data, though, but with lots of rows I'll generally stick with portrait orientation instead.

You'll have to decide what works best for you, your specific data, and where the printed document will be used.

Letter / Legal / Statement / Etc.

This is where you select your paper type. Unless you're in an office or overseas, chances are you'll leave this exactly like it is. I'm sure my printer could print on legal paper, but I don't have any for it to use so it's a moot point for me.

In an office you may have the choice of standard paper, legal paper, and even other larger sizes than that. Just make sure whatever you choose is in fact an available option for you.

Normal Margins / Wide Margins / Narrow Margins / Custom Margins

I would expect you won't use this, but if you need to then this would be where you can change the margins on the document. The normal margins allow for .7" on each side and .75" on top and bottom. If you have a lot of columns and need just a little more room to fit it all on one page, you could use the narrow margin option which uses .25" margins on the left and right.

I generally use the scaling option to do this instead.

No Scaling / Fit Sheet on One Page / Fit All Columns on One Page / Fit All Rows on One Page / Custom Scaling

I use this option often when I have a situation where my columns are just a little bit too much to fit on the page or my rows go just a little bit beyond the page.

If you choose "Fit All Columns on One Page" that will make sure that all of your columns fit across the top of one page.

You might still have multiple pages because of the number of rows, but at least everything will fit across one page.

Of course, depending on how many columns you have, this might not be a good choice. Excel will make it fit, but it will do so by decreasing your font size. If you have too many columns you're trying to fit on one page your font size may become so small you can't read it.

So be sure to look at your preview before you print. (And use Landscape Orientation first if you can.)

Fit All Rows on One Page is good for if you have maybe one or two rows too many to naturally fit on the page.

Fit Sheet on One Page is a combination of fitting all columns and all rows onto one page. Again, Excel will do it if you ask it to, but with a large set of data you won't be able to read it, so be careful making this choice.

I usually end up going with Custom Scaling. If you click on that option it opens the Page Setup dialogue box to the Page tab where you can go to the Scaling section and choose to Fit To X pages by Y pages. So maybe I have a report that is five pages long right now with only one row on that last page. I can use scaling to make this 1 page wide by 4 pages long and that will bring that last row up onto my fourth page and give me a cleaner print out than if I just left it as is.

Same with if I have a report that is currently fifteen pages long because the last column extends to the next page so I have ten pages with most of my information spread across two pages wide and five pages long but then I have another five pages with just that last column. I can set this to 2 pages wide by 5 pages long and bring that last column onto the second page.

(If you need it, play around with the setting and you'll see how it can help.)

Page Setup

The Page Setup link at the very bottom gives you access to even more options through the Page Setup dialogue box. We just talked about custom scaling. This is another way to reach that setting. You can also:

1. Center Horizontally or Vertically

On the Margins tab there are two check boxes that let you center what you're printing either horizontally or vertically or both. I will often choose to center a smaller data table horizontally. If I don't do that, it tends to look off balance.

2. Header/Footer

If you want to set up a header and/or a footer for your printed document, you can do so here. The dropdown boxes that say (none) include a number of pre-formatted headers and footers for you to use.

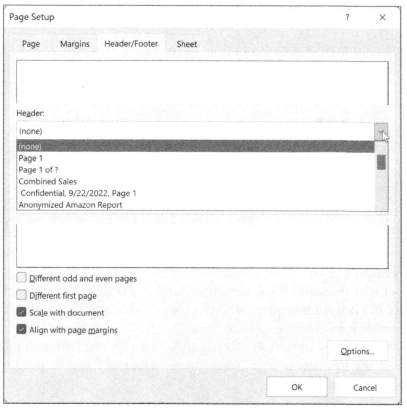

You can see here options for including the page number, worksheet name, and workbook name, for example. Each one shows an example of the actual text that will be included.

Not visible above, because the buttons are hidden behind the dropdown, are options for customizing the header and footer.

3. Sheet

The sheet tab has a couple of useful options, but I'm going to show you a different way to set these options because I find it easier to set them when I'm in the worksheet itself.

* * *

Page Layout Tab

If you exit out of the print option and go back to your worksheet, you'll see that one of the tabs you have available to use is called Page Layout. There are certain attributes that I set up here before I print my documents. Let's walk through them.

(First, though, note that you can change margins, orientation, and size here just as easily as in the print preview screen.)

1. Print Area

If you only want to print a portion of a worksheet, you can set that portion as your print area by highlighting it, and then clicking on the arrow next to Print Area and choosing Set Print Area.

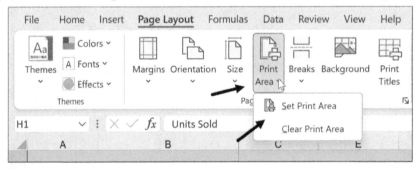

Only do it this way (as opposed to highlighting the section and choosing Print Selection) if it's a permanent setting.

Once you set your print area it will remain set until you clear it. You can add more data to your worksheet but it will never print until you change your print area, clear the setting, or deliberately override it when you choose to print.

I use this when I have a worksheet that has either a lot of extra information I don't want to print or where the formatting extends beyond my data and Excel keeps trying to print all those empty but formatted cells.

2. Breaks

You can set where a page break occurs in your worksheet. So say you have a worksheet that takes up four pages and you want to make sure that rows 1 through 10 are on a page together and then rows 11 through 20 are on a page together even though that's not how things would naturally fall. You can set a page break to force that to happen.

To insert a break, click on the cell where you want to insert the page break and then click on the dropdown for Breaks and choose Insert Page Break. You'll see a line appear on the worksheet to indicate where the page break is.

You can also use that dropdown to Reset All Page Breaks or remove a specific page break.

Personally, I find page breaks a challenge to work with, so I usually try to get what I need some other way.

3. Print Titles

This one is incredibly valuable. When you click on it, you'll see that it brings up the Page Setup box and takes you to the Sheet tab.

The first valuable thing you can do here is set the rows you want to repeat at the top of the page.

Say you have a worksheet with a thousand rows of data in it that will print on a hundred pages. How do you know what's in each column on each page? You need a header row. And you need that header row to repeat at the top of each and every page.

"Rows to repeat at top" is where you specify what row(s) is your header row. Click in that box and then select the row number(s) in your worksheet that you want to have repeat at the top of each page and Excel will write the cell notation for you. (This is why I do this in the worksheet itself instead of from the Print screen.)

The second valuable thing you can do here is set a column(s) you want to repeat on the left-hand side of each page. I need this one less often, but I do still sometimes use it.

Say, for example, that you had a list of students, one per row, and their test scores across fifty tests, and that when you printed that information it printed across two pages. Without listing the student's name in the left-hand column on every page, you wouldn't know whose scores you were looking at after the first page. But you can set that name column to repeat on each page.

To do so, click in the box that says "Columns to repeat at left", and then select the column(s) you want to repeat. Excel will once more write the cell notation you need for you in that field.

If you feel comfortable enough with cell notation you could do this from the print screen, but I never do.

You can repeat more than one row or column on each page, but if you do that, be careful that you don't end up selecting so many rows or columns to repeat that you basically just print the same thing over and over and over again. (Think of this as the printer equivalent of freeze panes if that helps.)

Okay. That's it. Let's wrap this up with a quick conclusion and then you're ready to dive in with using Excel.

Conclusion

As I explained at the beginning, this book was not meant to be comprehensive. Pick up one of the comprehensive books on Microsoft Excel and you'll see that it's two inches thick with small type.

Excel is insanely powerful, but most people don't need all of that. What I gave you here in this book is 95% of what you'll need day-to-day.

You can fill in the gaps as you go along using Excel's help function or online searches, or you can continue on with me in one of two directions if you want. (Or both, I won't mind.)

The next book in this series, *Intermediate Excel 365*, covers more advanced topics like pivot tables, charts, and conditional formatting that can be very valuable when analyzing data.

The other option is *102 Useful Excel 365 Functions*. That one covers exactly what you think it would: how to work with formulas and functions in Microsoft Excel. I've tried in that book to call out the functions I think are most useful. And I've mentioned a number of functions in passing that relate to those functions or are alternate versions of those functions.

For example, I talk about TEXTJOIN in there which allows you to join text strings. But I also cover the older functions that would let you do this, CONCATENATE and CONCAT.

But you don't have to stick with me and buy another book on these topics, because Excel has excellent help available. (The advantage my books give is they focus in specific areas and keep out the noise, so they provide a path to follow. But if you don't need the path, then you don't need a book. Anyway.)

You can open Help in Excel using F1. Or, as of now–this has changed over time–help is available by going to the Help tab at the top of the screen and then clicking on Help from there.

Either option in current versions of Excel will open a task pane on the right-hand side of the workspace that has a search bar as well as a number of help topics available.

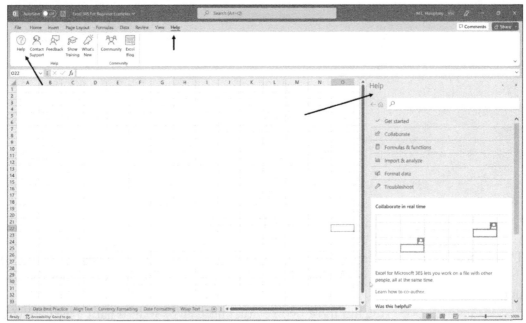

I often find it easier to click on Tell Me More which is available when you hover over specific options, like here with Format Painter.

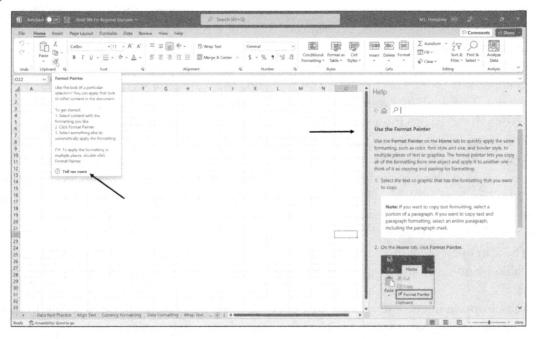

That always goes straight to the help topic for that particular option.

I will also often do a web search and then click on the link that goes to support.microsoft.com. So I might say, "microsoft excel copy formatting" and then click on the link that shows that it came from microsoft.

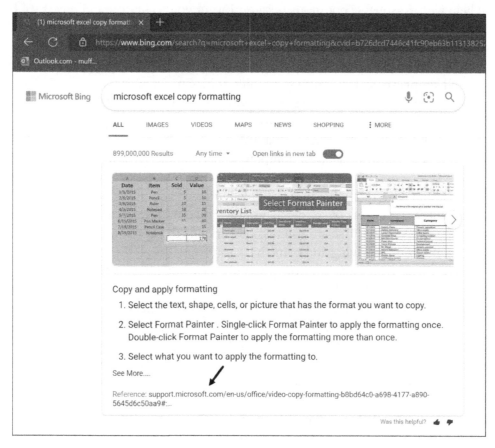

I've noticed in the last six months or so that at least the search engines I'm using give a fairly detailed preview of search results these days so that I don't even have to click through to a website sometimes to see the information I need. (Which is kind of crap for anyone who relies on ad revenue they generate from their website (which I don't), but that's the world for you. Always evolving, sometimes not in favor of the people who provide the value.)

Anyway. The Microsoft built-in help and website are both very good for when you need to know *how* to do something. "How do I copy an entry?", "How do I paste an entry?", "How does X function work?", etc.

For questions about "is this possible" they're less helpful. For that you either need to find someone who made a blog post or video doing what you want to do, or you need to wade into a tech forum somewhere and ask the experts how to do it.

You're always welcome to reach out to me with a question, too. Just know that if you start asking me to do your work for you, I'll quote you my (very expensive) consulting rates. I'm happy to clarify something or point you in the right direction, but "please build this complex calculation for me" is a step beyond that.

I will help with reasonable questions because I want you to understand this stuff, but also please respect that I can't do your work for you.

Also, know that there is no question that I will mock you for asking. I once had to train 90-year-old ladies on how to use a computer system so I know that people can be perfectly intelligent and simply struggle because something is new to them.

I try to keep in mind when I write these books what it's like to be new to Excel, but I sometimes miss something. For example, to click on the X in the top right corner to close things. Or to click on OK to be done with a dialogue box. These are things that are ingrained in me from decades of working with computers that I sometimes forget that other people don't know.

So ask what you need to ask because if I failed to teach you, that's on me.

Okay, that's it. I hope you now understand how powerful Excel can be. Don't be afraid to make mistakes. Ctrl + Z and Esc are you two best friends to get out of trouble. When all else fails, close the file without saving and come back to it.

If you're working with data for work maybe check out *How To Gather and Use Data for Business Analysis*, which is based on my lessons learned from working on data projects in a corporate setting. It talks about how to get data that you can effectively use for analysis.

If you want to understand how to apply basic math in Excel to budgeting then check out the *Juggling Your Finances: Basic Excel Guide*. It walks through Excel from the perspective of using addition, subtraction, multiplication, and division to calculate your basic financial status. (And is a companion to *Budgeting for Beginners* which explains how to use that information to improve your finances.)

You can find links to both of those at https://mlhumphrey.com/business-and-personal-finance/ and links to all of my Microsoft Office books (there are so many) at https://mlhumphrey.com/microsoft-office-all-links/.

And if there's something you need that I haven't written, let me know, I might write it. I wrote *Mail Merge for Beginners* because someone said they needed a book on that and I figured it was pretty easy for me to put it together for them.

Also if you tell me and I write it, chances are I'll send you a free ebook copy as a thank you. No guarantee I'll write it, but if I do…you get your question answered and I have another book out there that people may need. Win-win.

Okay. Good luck with it. Don't be scared. You can do this.

SHORTCUTS

The below tables contain various useful Excel shortcuts, most of which were discussed in the chapters of this book. The header row for each table shows which key to use and then the Task column tells you what that will accomplish. For example, Ctrl + N will open a new Excel file.

Ctrl +	Task
N	New File
O	Open File
S	Save File
C	Copy
V	Paste
X	Cut
Z	Undo
F	Open Find and Replace Dialogue Box to Find tab
A	Select All
P	Print
W	Close Current Workbook
B	Bold/Unbold Selected Text
I	Italicize/Remove Italics From Selected Text
U	Underline/Remove Underline From Selected Text
1	Open Format Cells Dialogue Box

Ctrl +	Task
End	Go to Last Column of Blank Worksheet OR Go to Last Column In Data Range OR Go to Next Column to the Right With Data
Home	Go to First Column of Blank Worksheet OR Go to First Column in Data Range OR Go to Next Column to the Left with Data
Down Arrow	Go to Last Row of Blank Worksheet OR Go to Last Row In Data Range OR Go to Next Row Down That Contains Data
Up Arrow	Go to First Row of Blank Worksheet OR Go to First Row In Data Range OR Go to Next Row Up That Contains Data
Right Arrow	Go to Last Column of Blank Worksheet OR Go to Last Column In Data Range OR Go to Next Column to the Right With Data
Left Arrow	Go to First Column of Blank Worksheet OR Go to First Column in Data Range OR Go to Next Column to the Left with Data

Alt +	Task
S	Refresh Pivot Table
H	Access Menu Options, Use Alt + Letter(s)/Number(s) to Select Task to Perform
Tab	Move Between Open Programs in Windows

Ctrl + Shift	Task
$	Format as Currency
#	Format as Date
!	Format as Number with Comma For Thousands
%	Format as Percent
Right Arrow	Select All Cells in Range To Right
Down Arrow	Select All Cells In Range Downward
Right and then Down Arrow	Select All Cells in Range Across and Down

Other	Task
Esc	Exit a Cell, Back Out of a Function, Close a Tool, General Escape Option
Tab	Move to the Right One Cell
Shift + Tab	Move to the Left One Cell
Windows Key + Ctrl + O	Open On-Screen Keyboard

Index

A

Addition 86

Align Text 95–96

Angle Text 96–97

Arrow keys 43

Arrow, Definition 21

Auto-Suggested Text 54–55

B

Bold Text 98

Borders Around Cells 98–102

    All Borders 104

    Clear 105

    Draw Border 103

    Draw Border Grid 100–101, 103

    Format Cells dialogue box 104–105

    Line Color 103, 105

    Line Style 102, 105

    Slanted line 105

Budget Worksheet 1

C

Cell Notation 81

    Columns 82

    Multiple Cells 81

    Rows 82

    Workbooks 82

    Worksheets 82

Cells

    Clear Formatting 60

    Color 105–107

    Copy Formatting 121–122

    Definition 18

    Delete 79

    Insert 78

Clear Formatting 122–123

Click, Definition 18

Close File 36

Color Text 113–114

Columns

    Definition 15–17

    Delete 79

    Hide 47

    Insert 76–77

    Unhide 48

    Width 107–108

Control Shortcuts

    Bold Text 98

    Close File 36

    Copy 66

    Currency Format 110

    Cut 68

    Date Format 112

    Find 61

    Move Between Workbooks 41

    Move Between Worksheets 42

    Move One Screen 43

    Move to End of Worksheet 44

    New File 31

    Number Format 118

    Open 35

    Open Format Cells Dialogue Box 95

    Paste 68

    Redo 53

    Replace 61

    Save 38

    Select All 65

    Shortcuts Listing 149–150

    Underline Text 119

    Undo 52

Copy 66–68

    Copy Formatting 121–122

    Copy Formulas 91–94

    Copy Patterns 55–57

Cursor Functions 21

Cut 68

D

Data

Definition 20

Delete 60

Edit 51

Enter 50

Select 65

Data Principles 49–50

Data Table, Definition 20–21

Date Format 110–112

Delete a File 39–40

Dialogue Boxes, Definition 24–25

Display as Text 58–59

Division 87

Dropdown Menus, Definition 22–23

E

Esc 53, 94

F

F2 51

File

Change Name 39

Close 36

Delete 39–40

Open 29–35

Save 36–38

File Naming Tip 40

Fill Color 105–107

Filtering 129–134

Find 60–61, 63

Font Choice 112

Font Color 113–114

Font Size 112–113

Format Cells Dialogue Box 95

Formula Bar, Definition 26

Formulas and Functions 83

Basic Math Calculations 86–87

Copying 91–92

Create a Formula 84

Examples 83

Fixed Cell References 93–94

Formula, Definition 83

Function, Definition 83

Moving 94

View Result 85

Where To Find Functions 88–91

Freeze Panes 44, 46

H

Help 23–24, 145–148

Hide Columns or Rows 47–48

I

Indent Text 114–115

Information. See Data

Italicize Text 115

L

Left-click and Drag 19, 26, 119

Left-click, Definition 19

Line Breaks 59

M

Mac Computers 1, 4

Merge & Center 115–116

Merge Across 116

Merge Cells 116

Mini Formatting Menu 95

Move 41

Between Excel Workbooks 41

Between Excel Worksheets 42

Data 66–67

Formulas 94

Within An Excel Worksheet 43

Worksheet 74

Multiplication 87

N

Number Format 116

Comma Style 117–118

Currency 108–109

Decrease Decimal 118

Increase Decimal 118

Number 117

Percent 118

Scientific 117

O

Office 365 4–5

Office Theme 9–13

On Premise Version 4

Online Version 3

Open File 29–35

P

Paste 66–67

Paste Special 69–71

    Paste Transpose 71–72

    Paste Values 71–72

Pin A File 35

Printing 135

    Center 141

    Collation 138

    Fit to Page 140

    Header/Footer 141

    Margins 139

    Number of Copies 137

Orientation 139

Page Breaks 142

Paper Size 139

Print Area 142

Printer Selection 137

Repeat Rows or Columns 143–144

Two-Sided 138

What To Print 137–138

R

Redo 53

Repeated Entries 55–57

Replace 60–63

Right-click, Definition 19

Rows

    Definition 17–18

    Delete 79

    Height 118–119

    Hide 47

    Insert 76–77

Unhide 48

S

Save File 36–38

Scroll Bars 44

    Definition 25–26

Scroll Lock 64

Select All 65–66

Select, Definition 19–20

Sorting 125–129

Subtraction 87

T

Tab key 43

Tabs, Definition 21–22

Task Pane, Definition 26–27

U

Underline Text 119

Undo 52

W

Workbook, Definition 15

Worksheets

Add 73

Copy 75

Definition 15

Delete 76

Move 74

Move Between 42

Rename 72–73

See All 43

Selected 42

Wrap Text 119–121

About the Author

M.L. Humphrey is a former stockbroker with a degree in Economics from Stanford and an MBA from Wharton who has spent close to twenty years as a regulator and consultant in the financial services industry.

You can reach M.L. at mlhumphreywriter@gmail.com or at mlhumphrey.com.

Made in United States
North Haven, CT
27 May 2024

53012704R00091